White Cats & Lilacs

Teresa Keene

White Cats & Lilacs

Teresa Keene

Howell Press

Edited by Katherine A. Neale,
Louisa Tyson Whitman, and Ross A. Howell, Jr.
Designed by Carolyn Weary Brandt

Printed in the United States of America
Published by Howell Press, Inc., 1147 River Road, Suite 2,
Charlottesville, Virginia 22901.
Telephone (804) 977-4006.
First Printing

HOWELL PRESS

Library of Congress Cataloging-in-Publication Data
Keene, Teresa, 1962-
        Whites cats and lilacs / by Teresa Keene.
p. cm.
ISBN: 1-57427-060-5.

1. Gardening.   I. Title
SB450.97.K44 1996   635
                                     QBI96-20231

For my wonderful grandmother, Mildred Downey Trail,
who has gone to that great lilac grove in the sky,
and to Alvin Doctor, otherwise known as "Doc," "Al," "Dad," and "Papa."
You two planted the seeds.

Contents

Acknowledgments

he author gratefully acknowledges the following people, without whose splendid minds and hearts this book would not exist:

Sandra Kosmalski, editor of *The Cowboy Country Express*, sweet friend, and southern lady extraordinaire. Thank you, darlin', for publishing my first gardening column and the forty or so that came later!

The Washington State University Master Gardeners, sponsored by the Kitsap County Cooperative Extension, whose wonderful training and volunteer opportunities brought my love of gardening into focus.

My cheerleading squad: my patient husband John, who also provided the artwork for this book; my mother Phyllis Doctor, who brags about me to everyone at work; my adorable sisters Terril Moore and Lindy Bullard, who said, "Hey, even if you only sell five books it's still cool!"; my sweet sons Josh and Alex for enthusiastically not bugging me while I was at the computer; and my best friend Terri, who calmed me down whenever I got a bad case of stage fright. You guys are the best.

Preface

y love of writing goes way back to that day in 1968, when—at age six—I wrote my mother a poem for her birthday. It wasn't much of a poem, but she enjoyed it, although I suspect that this was mainly due to relief at not having received her own shabby eight-year-old handbag again. (That is what I had given her the year before, after digging it out of the attic and wrapping it proudly in Sunday's comics.)

My love of gardening, as you will learn in the following essays, goes almost as far back, though I didn't realize that love was the word for it until after I grew up and started a family. After several years of trial and error, extensive reading, failure and success, I applied for the Washington State University Master Gardeners program through my local cooperative extension. Their serious approach to the business end of gardening, together with the many hours of community gardening service required for certification, filled in most of the technical gaps in my horticultural knowledge.

The most important thing I brought away with me, I believe, is something they drilled into our heads every week: It's not terrifically important that you memorize every horticultural detail known to man; it is, however, of utmost importance to know how to look things up. It is a skill not to be sneezed at, I've learned. Nearly any gardening challenge can be overcome if you know the right place to look for the answers. This has been invaluable advice.

WHITE CATS & LILACS is not a book of expert advice on gardening. I carry no degrees in the field. I wrote the essays you now hold one at a time, for a small but heartfelt Texas newspaper. I wrote them because I love gardening, and because I wanted to help other people appreciate and love it, too. Not only do I get a kick out of playing in the dirt, but it gives me a lift to look at my property and see what my two hands (and my husband's!) can do. But more importantly, I really hope to make a difference in what other people's properties look like.

Drive down any street, and you will see grass. Endless, green, wasteful grass. I truly believe there is too much of it. It consumes too much water in this day and age of conservation. It requires, in mowing, fertilizing, thatching, and seeding, far too much of our precious time and resources. People, in Herculean efforts to keep their grass emerald green, pour insecticides and herbicides and other chemicals all over it. The rain washes these chemicals down our storm drains and into our creeks and rivers. People who live by the sea, a lake, or a river are no longer surprised when they hear of mysterious fish die-offs every spring. Is it coincidence that these die-offs generally occur after the initial spring rush to the local garden centers for lawn additives?

But flower gardening is different. Mulch the beds nicely once a year and they require very little water. Plant perennials once and you generally will never have to plant them again. Make your own compost and they will not need fertilizers. They have a few pests, but these pests are usually kept in control by the beneficial pests that gobble them up before they do much damage, negating a real need for pesticides. Weeding is minimal if, once again, one mulches.

But these are all just practical reasons to garden. In the end, it is the sheer relief of spying the first crocus after a long winter that provides the most pleasure. It is the sigh of satisfaction evoked when you walk past lilacs blooming in May. It is the fun of watching a cat roll in the catnip you planted in the corner of the dahlia bed. It is the ugly foundation hidden by the daylilies, the worn-out fence brightened by climbing roses, the stark squares of your windows fluffed up from below by cascading window boxes.

But most of all, it is what happens within a family that shares gardening with one another. Children planting seeds and watching what happens, grandmothers snapping beans with grandchildren, husbands working in the bright sun with wives they see little of during the work week, fathers and mothers battling the elements to turn something stark into a thing of beauty they can surround their children with.

I was inspired to garden by many people and things. I would like this book to be one of the small things that inspires you to garden, too.

Teresa Keene
March 14, 1996

White Cats & Lilacs

My first gardening experience involved a big white cat and lilacs. When I was small, my grandmother had a white, tomato-eating cat. Grandma, a great admirer of cats, always gave them respectable names. The tomato-eater was christened Mrs. Murphy, and she was huge, weighing in at a muscle-bound twenty-eight pounds.

My grandfather contended that cats were, in fact, aliens, pointing out their yellow eyes, independent habits, and sometimes bizarre behavior as proof. This particular cat didn't do much to change his mind.

Mrs. Murphy would steal amongst the grapevines, potato vines, and cabbages to the back of the garden where my grandmother's tomatoes, trussed up like leafy dungeon people, warily dwelled. She would carefully select the choicest, ripest fruit of the day and swat it around like a mouse, finally giving it one good left hook. Mrs. Murphy would scarf down the bleeding victim enthusiastically, growling and switching her tail. She was sure that an interloping cat hid in the lilacs, waiting to steal the tomato away from her. But, the neighborhood felines did not share Mrs. Murphy's grand passion for the sun-ripened fruit.

Now, many gardeners would have reacted poorly to such a cat, giving in to their baser natures by shooing or even kicking it away. But my grandmother, a tough old country woman with a droll sense of humor, considered Mrs. Murphy a conversation piece and grist for her understated wit. She simply planted extra tomato plants each spring.

"Mrs. Murphy," she once remarked dryly after watching a particularly animated display, "are you ready for a cigarette now?"

The garden was big. Hedged in on three sides by gigantic old lilacs, it was the larger part of a half-acre lot in Spokane, Washington. I remember being enveloped by the sweet smell of the lilacs in the late spring as I wandered around in the dirt, watching Grandma and Mrs. Murphy go about their business. Spokane is known as "The City of Lilacs," although I didn't know that then. Mrs. Murphy herself was lilac-scented in the spring, and no matter where I went, that aroma seemed to follow. I simply assumed that it had rubbed off on me, too.

Now I live on the other side of the state, where lilacs grow, certainly, although their fragrance does not follow one farther than a few feet from the bush. And cats invade gardens, but they do things there that Grandma's otherwise well-mannered Mrs. Murphy never dreamed of. I have never again encountered a tomato-eating cat.

Yet, I took away two lifelong loves from those spring days in that garden. To this day, I own lots of lilacs. And, thanks to a large, white, scarlet-stained, lilac-scented feline, I have an enduring weakness for eccentric cats.

Bleakness, Beauty, & Bills

We bought an old house last winter with an equally old apple orchard. Suckers and water sprouts burst forth from the gnarled branches with rhapsodic eagerness, but we quickly cut their exuberance short by pruning them. The old trees resembled colossal bonsai, and were lovely in their stark way.

All the same, I found the orchard to be a pretty bleak place when late winter and early spring arrived. While everybody else's property was gloriously covered in crocus, camellias, and snowdrops, my apple orchard came in last in the local spring beauty pageant. The apple trees did not bloom until May, and then only sparsely, due to the severe haircut I had given them.

How many times did I gaze out my window at that barren half of my acreage, wishing for some sign of life? Countless times, but from October through most of May, it remained bare and brown. I formulated a plan.

I took up my numerous bulb catalogs that May and greedily consumed their contents. One catalog, promising that I wouldn't have to pay until my shipment arrived, especially touched my heart. With no money worries to stop me, I became a carefree lady of leisure and ordered $500.00 worth of bulbs.

October first arrived, and so did my shipment: box after box of tulips, daffodils for naturalizing, crocus, snow irises, muscari, hyacinths, snowdrops, and giant jonquils. My husband and I spent two days carefully planting one thousand bulbs in and around that orchard, knowing the flowers and leaves would get all the sunlight they needed before the trees leafed up at the end of May. I am expecting a wonderland there, beginning in February.

But, oh gosh, the bill. Suddenly I don't feel like a carefree lady of leisure who need merely dash off a check with wealthy abandon. I feel like some poor slob who bought a new car she couldn't afford from a charming salesman, a salesman who promised no payments until October! In October, I swore I'd pay it in November. In November, I vowed I'd pay it in December.

Well, December is here, and so is Christmas, and my folly is evident in the angry reminders from the bulb company, which will probably never sell to me again. Oh, I'll pay them all right. In January, for sure. But still, I can't wait to see my orchard burst into life come crocus time with those harbingers of spring. And by March, I'm sure that $500.00 will have been worth it. That is, if the gophers don't get those bulbs first.

Pessimism & Optimism

When we bought our old farmhouse so cheaply last year, we went on and on about how lucky we were to get it at such an amazing price. Of course, after living in the place for one month it was all too clear why it was cheap. The basement flooded every fall. The house was a maze of poor repairs, bad wiring, and even worse plumbing. We no longer considered ourselves lucky, just resigned. But as bad as the house was, the landscaping was worse.

The orchard hadn't been pruned in years. Gophers had crisscrossed the yard with tunnels. I broke my ankle stepping into one of their holes while planting roses last spring. The cedars, lilacs, maples, and hawthorns were all so hopelessly overgrown and sick that we had to hire a tree man to climb up there and operate. The two tall camellia trees, although they displayed promisingly fat buds on their glossy leaves in January, had revealed February blooms that were brown with blight. A thirty-five-foot holly tree leaned like the Tower of Pisa in front of the house and the rhododendron bed on the north side had been dug into deep pits by the previous owner's dog.

All of this dismayed me, but gardeners are optimists by nature. How else is it possible for us to plant bulbs knowing that rodents will eat them? How else is it conceivable for us to plant new roses after an unexpected cold snap kills the old ones? So I focus on the good points.

I cherish the huge, rambling old rosebush, which no disease or temperature extreme can touch, that sits in the southwest corner of the property. Its tiny white blooms, swirling around it by the thousands in June, smell delicately of hand lotion.

The holly, though it leans, is covered with scarlet berries all winter and sits right outside my living room window.

The cedars smell divine, and the gigantic rhododendrons in that ravaged north bed are immune to the destructive efforts of dogs; they bloom exuberantly in hues of fuchsia and lavender.

A surprise crop of red and white peonies popped up in the grass last spring, and I thanked God I spied them before I mowed them down.

All of which leaves me with one small piece of advice. If you buy or inherit a seemingly hopeless garden, don't call in the bulldozers to tear everything up just yet. Wait a year. Watch what happens. There are forces beneath your feet that may be slumbering for now. Just give them a little time to wake up.

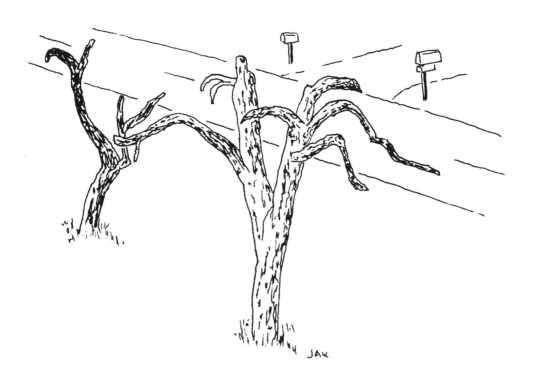

Making Something
out
of Nothing

oday I am visiting my father's three-acre garden in the hills up
north.

When I was small, it was a three-acre farm, but before that it was a
three-acre mess filled with stumps, ten-foot-high brambles, rotten fallen
timbers, and rocks. It was situated on a hillside between two deep gullies.
Giant electric cables were strung from one tower to the next over the
whole eastern half of the property. The towers looked like colossal paper
dolls.

When my father first saw the place, he did not complain. He is an
outdoorsman, having earned his living for most of his life in the forests of
the Pacific Northwest and in construction. This three-acre plot was all he
had at the time, and he decided he would make it support his family.

He got out his chain saw and sawed up the old logs into firewood.
He burned up the brambles, day after day. My sisters and I were enlisted to
"pick" rocks, a pastime we did not especially like, but of course did anyway. That plot was rich with rocks, and there must have been some special
rock fertilizer in the soil because every year it produced new and bigger
rocks, poking their noses out of the soil in the spring the way daffodils do.

My father built a barn, a pump house, a garage, a shop, a pigpen, a
chicken coop, a corral, lots of fencing, and front and back porches for our
little house. He raised veal calves for market, milk cows for our dairy needs
(and for more calves), hogs, chickens, ponies for me, ducks, you name it.

He cultivated a big vegetable garden by the barn where he grew every vegetable a large family could need. And he did it all with hardly any money, a twice-broken back, and a foot that doctors said he would never walk on again—a statement he scoffed at and proved a lie. He's rugged, an old-fashioned tough guy. And that place fed us well, no matter how little money we had.

But as finances improved and we kids moved away, Dad decided he didn't need to grow all that food anymore. So the tough guy turned the farm into a garden. And golly, by then the soil was so fertile he could've grown anything there. The pigpen is now an orchard that produces more fruit per tree than I have ever seen.

A horseshoe pit has replaced the corral. He planted Christmas trees all over the pasture and lets the Boy Scouts come and take them every year for their fundraiser. He's raised silver birches, ornamental plums, cherry trees, and tall leafy ashes from twigs he planted twenty-five years ago.

Rhododendrons and lilies-of-the-valley now roam where my stubborn pony Koko used to graze, and beautiful wood carvings of bears, trout, elves, and raccoons made by an artisan friend of Dad's dot every flower bed.

I look at the place and know what I am seeing. The garden is a three-acre reflection of my father, adapted from hardscrabble to productive, from productive to serene. It is the testimony of a man who still finds good in a hard life, a man who can make a garden out of rocks.

Successful Ignorance

My first garden was an accidental success. It scares me to think of how haphazard I was: I planted lime lovers next to acid lovers, put tall plants in front of short ones, tucked sun lovers into shady nooks. I naïvely put plants that needed good drainage and little water in clay pockets under the downspout, and flora that should have been kept wet and soggy I planted at the top of sandy slopes.

It's amazing how well that garden did!

My garden was basically the small front and back yards of the first house we ever owned, a thirteen-hundred-square-foot rambler in a 1972 subdivision. All the topsoil had been scraped away by bulldozers when the subdivision was built, leaving nothing but sandy soil with lots of rocks and a few clayey deposits.

I robustly (I was only twenty-six) dug up most of my grass for four years, double-digging two-foot-deep holes in various shapes and sizes. My all-purpose garden solution—the only one I knew at the time—was to mix in bales of peat moss and let it go at that. It didn't occur to me to add fertilizer or lime, manure or chips. One soil fits all, I figured.

Then, in my happy ignorance, I would order everything I liked out of my catalogs, without planning or forethought. Plant blues, pinks, and purples together for a more balanced color scheme? Pshaw! I virtuously pointed to God's rainbow and told myself, "All of Mother Nature's colors go together!"

Keep acid-loving camellias with the other evergreens and away from the daylilies? Forget it! I visualized creamy yellow daylilies springing up in front of the dark green camellia leaves, proudly using the contrast to show off their glow. In fact, according to the garden books I am such a maven of now, I committed just about every gardening error of form, style, and function a person can commit.

But guess what. That was a simply beautiful garden. Everything grew. Monarda flourished next to red-hot poker, rhododendrons and camellias thrived with the daylilies and Queen Anne's lace. Cosmos seeds scattered randomly throughout a bed of perennials took hold there and beautifully covered up the end-of-the-summer blahs. An azalea sprung vividly out of a mat of supposedly choking creeping thyme I had planted around it, as did my daffodils from out of a mat of mint.

I only learned one thing from that garden, but it is the most important thing: Don't be guided by books on style when you plan your garden. In fact, don't plan period, if you can help it. Plants have a way of surprising you. They are flexible, strong, persistent, and stubborn. I find that most flowers do their worst when I give them the most attention.

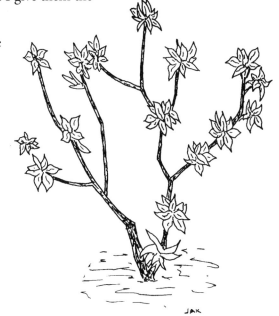

Just give them a place to grow, a little love, and a little water when they're thirsty, and they'll do just fine. Who knows? Accidental success may be yours, too, someday.

Moon Gardens
& Dreams

Lately I've been thinking that a white garden would be a heavenly thing to have. A Moon Garden. A garden that, if planted before the lush green backdrop of the horse pasture on the hill behind the house, would certainly be lovely by day. But by night, ah, yes, by night it would glow with a radiant light of its own.

The moon garden of my dreams glows with a shimmery, surreal incandescence even when the sky is overcast. But when our night-sky visitor is gleaming down on my moon garden, I have great faith that its light will wax my flowers into a high sheen.

First I will till up the grass growing in that favored location. The spot is perfect because my moon flowers will receive plenty of sunlight by day. I will add only the best to my heavy soil, lightening it with a little sand, providing fresh humus with some finished compost, throwing in a wheelbarrowful of horse manure for its nitrogen, and adding a little sweat from my brow for good luck. I will work and work this soil until it is perfect.

In February and March I will plant the spring and summer bloomers. Some 'Lace Handkerchief' irises, white but with lovely lavender and gold markings, shasta daisies for their strong, wild appeal, and white bleeding hearts, which I will plant next to some low-growing creeping phlox. In the moon garden of my dreams, the bleeding hearts drip and hang romantically over the phlox like an ardent suitor.

In the back of the bed I will lovingly plant a dozen hollyhocks, where they will tower majestically just behind the two or three 'John F. Kennedy' roses. The JFK's blossoms will be highlighted against not only their own foliage, but the foliage of the hollyhocks behind them. I will toss lupines in the middle somewhere, as well as Canterbury bells, a few daylilies, and some chrysanthemums. I believe I will flank the bed with 'Annabelle' hydrangeas.

Of course everything will be brilliantly white.

Next fall I will plant bulbs under the perennials. White Darwin tulips for their hardiness and size, white daffodils, white muscari, white giant hyacinths, white oriental lilies. Snowdrops, too, and of course, crocus.

And I will go out into my garden by day and enjoy the red roses on the north fence. I will smile at the orange and yellow and pink dahlias crashing over the sidewalk next to the garage. I will even sigh happily at the white garden just this side of the pasture fence. But at night . . .

Yes, yes. I will walk out on a crisp spring night and marvel at the crocus and daffodils. On a balmy summer's eve I will sit in an old deck chair strategically placed in the center of my moon garden and relish the roses and lilies and hollyhocks while they shine as if lit from within. The moon will shimmer down on them and on me and I will thank God for allowing me to fiddle with His nature just enough to make something like this.

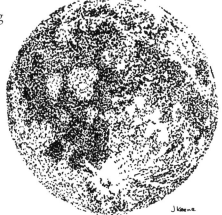

I will lean back amidst this swirl of organic light and count my blessings.

A Passionate Woman
vs. the Un-Gardeners

If you have a passion for anything, you know about "them."
Their eyes glaze over when you talk about your passion. They get peeved when you cancel a visit to work on it. They won't give it the attention and admiration it deserves when you show it off to them. Whether your passion is pedigreed poodles, fine wine, Star Trek, or gardening, you no doubt know them. They are the "Uns": Un-gardeners. Un-dog lovers. Un-Trekkers.

I have had countless encounters with un-gardeners, and they are different. Most people, although not always as passionate about gardening as I am, at least appreciate the passion itself, having one of some sort or another themselves. Not the un-gardeners. I've discovered that they generally have no ruling interest in anything. They make me crazy!

There was such a fellow who lived in my neighborhood many years ago. Every fall, the bulbs I had ordered the previous spring would inevitably arrive on the rainiest day of the year. Anxious to get them in the ground, I would find myself on my knees in my muddy flower beds planting them despite the downpour. Soaked to the skin and shivering, I enjoyed myself just the same. Without fail, the man in question would mosey down the street and stand at the curb, watching me from under a big umbrella.

"Ha ha ha," he'd laugh, pointing. "Ha ha ha ha HA! Are you nuts?"

"Hello, you old so-and-so," I'd mutter.

"Say!" he'd exclaim, imagining himself witty to no end. I knew what was coming. He said the same thing every year. I mouthed the words along with him. "I've got a dinghy in my garage you can float around in while you work!"

"Ha ha," I'd reply dryly, rolling my eyes.

"Why don't you wait for a sunny day, huh?" I'd jam my trowel into the dirt viciously. Déjà vu all over again.

"Because it is October in the Pacific Northwest," I'd respond calmly, "and if I waited for a sunny day to accomplish anything, I would never get anything done."

"Ha ha ha!" he'd say, shaking his head and pointing again. "You gardeners!" And he'd stroll back up Clueless Street from whence all "Uns" come. Once, I threw a bulb at the back of his head as he left.

"Thanks!" he said, smiling as he bent over to pick it up. "My pet rat will love this!"

I heard barking one day, and looked out the window towards my orchard. A strange woman stood on the shoulder of the road, watching indulgently as her Great Danes frolicked among the daffodils I had so carefully planted under the apple trees. I dashed outside just in time to see one of them do something rude right on top of a clump of blue grape hyacinths.

"Hey!" I yelled, outraged. The woman turned her smiling face toward me. She lifted up a hand encased in a plastic baggie.

"Don't worry," she called, "I'll pick it up." Scowling, I pulled my flagpole from out of its bracket on the wall next to my front door and ran down the steps, charging at the dogs as they trampled a patch of white 'Mt. Hood' daffodils. "Get!" I hollered. "Get out!"

The dogs stopped in their tracks, staring at me in surprise. I poked one in the ribs, and it yelped. "Bob!" the woman shouted, alarmed now. "Dennis! Come!" The dogs dashed over a forsythia bush, sending little golden florets flying. She turned on me. "How dare you!" she yelled.

"Me?" I squeaked. "Your stupid dogs are trampling my flowers!"

"I'll sue you if Bob is injured," she rejoined, pointing her baggied finger at me.

"These plants cost me $300.00," I replied, shaking. "Who will sue who?"

"Well," she huffed, turning and beginning to walk away.

"Pick up that poop!" I said. She came back and dourly scooped it up, turning the plastic neatly over the stuff.

"Some people!" she said. "I swear!"

To her retreating back I said, "At least I don't have dogs named Bob and Dennis!"

One day I was manning the master gardener's advice table in the nursery section of the local hardware store. A woman walked up to me holding a flat of impatiens.

"Can I help you?" I asked.

"Yes. What are these?"

"Impatiens," I told her. "They need to be planted in the shade."

She frowned. "But the place where I want to plant them is sunny all day."

I shrugged. "They'll die if you put them in a sunny place," I said. "Sorry."

She squinted at me. "What do *you* know?" she said, and headed toward the cash registers with the plants. My partner and I looked at each other. "I don't know," I said. "What *do* we know?"

"I don't know," responded my partner. "Do you know how to sing 'Danny Boy'?"

"I know that one," I said. We relaxed. We did know something.

I was buying a car last year. While filling out the loan application, the salesman asked, "What do you do?"

"I'm a writer," I said.

"Income?"

"Er—"

"What else?"

"Master gardener?" I said hopefully.

"And that is—?"

"Well, I volunteer for—"

"Housewife," he said, scribbling. And there I was, on paper for the entire credit-checking world to see, reduced to housewife because my passions didn't pay enough to earn recognition from what was obviously a passionless man!

As a woman with a passion, I've gritted my teeth so many times I'm surprised that they're not cracked and loose in my head. For although I know we must ignore the "Uns" no matter how much they test our patience, it is sometimes difficult.

I've decided that one must cultivate a sense of humor about the whole thing. The "Uns" don't mean any harm. Like a blind left fielder without a mitt, they're never going to get it.

Ungrateful Roses

A t this new house I wanted roses. Lots of them.

You see, at my old house, that dear little rambler in town, I had collected almost forty different rosebushes. They were all over the place; trained on the ugly chain link fence in the backyard, draped over the picket fence in the front yard, planted in a group under a terrible old cedar that leaned and gave them more shade than they wanted. But my space was limited, so I put them where I could. And I loved them.

I had all the best varieties that modern hybridizers could create: 'Peace,' 'Just Joey,' 'Double Delight,' 'Snowfire,' 'Angel Face,' 'Blaze,' 'Tropicana,' 'Bing Crosby,' and many more. There was just one problem— they needed to be coddled like babies.

My goodness, but they were demanding. I had to make sure they had an inch of water a week. That meant building little wells of dirt around each rose so that when I watered them the water would sink down to the roots and not run off.

They needed to be fed every two weeks, but talk about biting the hand that feeds you! I would reach under them and they would scratch me like surly cats. I wound up spending almost a whole day, twice a month, suffering the eighty-five- or ninety-degree heat in long sleeves and falconer's gloves.

They got whiteflies and aphids constantly, causing my darling roses' leaves to curl. Buds affected by these pests were shrimpy little things, opening up deformed if at all. This meant a weekly spraying program, and if I forgot even once, the tiny creatures were back with a vengeance. I tried a systemic fertilizer that doubled as an insecticide around the roots, but that didn't deter the whiteflies at all.

And the mildew! Once a little water or rain got on their leaves, powdery white mildew developed, especially on the roses that were placed in the shade or too close to the house or a fence and didn't get good air circulation. This meant a special mildew-preventing spray early in the spring before the plants leafed out, and every two weeks thereafter. It was all enough to make a person want to give up on roses.

So when we got this old house with its large yard I thought, "There are no roses here! I must have some!" But the other part of me that hated the fuss whispered, "With this big old shack and this big old yard and the kids and your writing, you'll never have time. You'll never keep up." I sighed sadly and resigned myself.

But then I received my Springhill Perennial catalog! And joy of joys, they offered a rose that resisted drought and cold, was pest-free, never needed pruning, grew on its own roots, and bloomed all summer! Ecstatically, I ordered sixty (at only $3.00 apiece) and planted them along the fence.

My Freedom roses grew like crazy: six feet tall. In summer they became a big, lovely, red-studded hedge that bloomed constantly. They fulfilled every promise. So now I have roses here. But, unlike my other bad-tempered hybrids at the old house, they don't have me!

February & Promise

February is almost here. February, a month of weighty promise for hopeful gardeners everywhere in this geographically diverse country. At one point during this month, in the damp darkness of an unseasonably warm and rainy night, daffodil and hyacinth noses push heroically through the soil to expose one tiny, rounded half-inch of green. One dare not step on one's bulb beds in February without looking very carefully first.

In February, if you look closely at your hydrangea, you see past the sad, leafless, fleshy arms that push up from the crown of the plant, and spy tender green buds, afraid to open just yet, dotting the length of each branch. Dead leaves, black and slimy, litter the ground around it. But the hydrangea lives, and waits for spring, its tiny sprouts quivering like horses at the starting gate.

By February, all the leaves have also fallen off the roses, but tiny red promises of tomorrow cling to the branches, and it is now that you must fulfill your duty to the rose by pruning it. I don't believe in pruning roses in the fall, as some do, for the *Rosa* needs every little bit of sun it can gather in its leaves for as long as it can to produce the best blossoms the next spring. No, wait until expectant February, and snip away the top two-thirds of the canes, being careful to cut them at a slant, directly above a leaf bud.

Many people despise February. It is like Thursday to them: so close to the weekend, yet not close enough. The chances for snow are likely to be nil, yet it is cold enough and wet enough to make some people miserable. But those people don't look for the signs as gardeners do. The hints of spring, the pledge of warmth, the vow that color and life will soon return.

So, can you hope? Can you appreciate what nature is doing? Can you see the signs? If you find yourself moping through short yet seemingly endless February, can Mother Nature lift your spirits? She can, but only if you let her.

Walk out in the cool, slanting sunlight and look around you. See the new greens of the bluebonnets just emerging? See the crocus as their blooms begin to push past their impatient leaves? See the buds fattening on the camellias? They will open before the month is out.

February is beautiful. Birds are singing earlier. Evening is coming later. March is a few short weeks away. Every living thing—feel it?—is trembling in anticipation. As am I.

JAK

On Being Young & Foolish

nce upon a time, I had a little house that had known no love for goodness knows how many years. Fences slowly rotted in place, the grass had made a strategic retreat, moss clambered excitedly over the roof, stumps of cruelly murdered flowering plum trees dotted the landscape.

But in my mind the saddest thing of all was the back patio.

It was obvious that, at one time in the distant past, someone had loved it. A thousand large bricks, now cracked and mildewy, formed the floor. Four-by-four treated posts stood tall, supporting a roof latticed with two-by-two boards. A lonely grapevine popped out of the high grass and tried to rest its weary head on a half-rotten trellis, which hung limply from the posts. Handmade benches, now peeling paint and listing, sat cozily between the posts.

Oh, but it was a gray and gloomy place.

I didn't have much money to work with. Fortunately, I was very young and didn't know yet that one must have a lot of money in order to create beauty. Foolish girl that I was, I actually believed I could make that patio lovely again with about twenty dollars.

My motto: A Can Of Paint Can Fix Anything. I painted every inch of wood with brilliant white paint: on sale for $4.00.

My other motto: Work With What You've Got. Those large bricks, which I priced at the hardware store, would cost me $1.39 each to replace.

So, since the mildew was too firmly imbedded and stubbornly refused to wash off, I simply turned them all over: a thousand 6" x 13" bricks, one at a time. The cracked ones remained cracked, but now that a new, shiny pink side faced up, the cracks looked rather charming. I absolutely had to replace three bricks because they were literally in pieces. The cost: about $4.20.

Yet another motto: Scrounge Through The Garage. In my garage I found a hideous old coffee table so ugly that even St. Vincent De Paul's wouldn't take it. I painted it bright red with leftover paint—also from my garage—and placed it in the corner of the patio. Two peeling chairs joined it after I painted them yellow. More garage junk.

Then I looked at my patio with a discerning eye. It needed plants. I ordered two silver-lace vines, at $2.00 apiece, from a catalog. They were

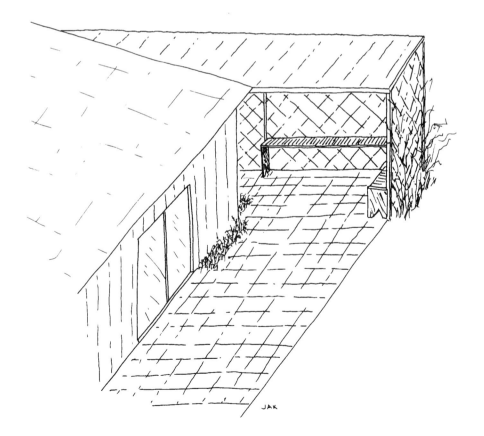

only three inches high, but they grew fifteen feet that first year and covered the trellises most satisfactorily. A neighbor rescued an old-fashioned climbing rose from a friend who had pulled it up to throw it away. Her mother-in-law had pruned it badly out of spite, so, out of spite, the daughter-in-law wanted it out of her sight. It covered one side of my trellis with pink blooms the next year.

I pulled up two bricks and planted marigold seeds ($1.20) in the dirt underneath. They spilled boisterously out of the patio floor. I scrounged up all the old pots I could find, painted (of course) the ones that weren't made of clay, filled them with garden dirt (potting soil was too expensive), and dug up whatever plants were in bloom. These I would rotate through my patio pots throughout the growing season, sticking them back in the ground when their bloom was done.

At last, it was a most satisfactory patio. And I still scratch my head when I look at the photos we took of it. Dear God, it was beautiful. And it only cost $14.40.

But of course, I was only twenty-six, and didn't know any better.

Puppies, Porches, & Plots

he idea for a front porch started when we bought a new puppy. Oh, we already had a full-grown Dalmatian, two cats, and two kids, but when we added Peaches the puppy to the equation it all added up to muddy floors tracked-up beyond belief. Being a gardener, I contributed greatly to the dirt, but that puppy was the last straw.

Peaches digs. She digs, digs, digs, digs, and digs some more. She even dug up the waterline to the house. I cannot seem to keep her from digging.

So I said to my husband, "You know, if we had a front porch, it would get the worst of the dirt off the dogs' feet before they came in, and our hardwood floors wouldn't need mopping quite so often." Of course, this argument didn't work, as it correctly sounded like I wanted to spend about $5,000 in order to avoid extra housework.

But it planted a seed. I worked away at him. I pointed out how one cannot stick one's head out the door during a storm without getting drenched. I pointed out that a covered front porch, spreading the width of the house, would be a charming addition to our home. I mentioned how the sun streaming into the living room was fading our furniture, and that a covered porch outside would block the sun. I noted that everyone always came around to the back door because no sidewalk or entry to our front door was visible from the driveway.

All of that helped, but the clincher was when I halfheartedly mentioned, without any hope of success, that I could fence off the front area to keep the dogs out and surround the porch and its new sidewalk with a cottage garden.

My husband's eyes, believe it or not, brightened. Shrewdly recognizing that I had touched on a seldom-seen love of beauty, I hastened to my stacks of gardening books and showed him pictures of enchanting farmhouses with covered front porches. Climbing roses trellised up their charming pillars. Large vibrant perennials crowded around quaint brick pathways. Baskets of bougainvillea and fuchsias hung from the rafters. My husband blinked. I knew I had him.

"Can you do that?" he asked, turning what I like to think of as a reverent gaze upon me.

"Certainly," I responded huffily. "What kind of gardener do you take me for?" I stalked away, but rubbed my hands together like the villain in a melodrama as soon as I was out of sight. The porch would be nice to have, I realized, but the cottage garden! Oh my, the cottage garden!

So, plans are being drawn up for the porch. Steps, beams, floorboards, shingles, yada, yada, yada. Who cares? I get to plant a great big cottage garden!

Yes, the wiles of the determined gardener are many and varied. So varied, in fact, that the gardener herself may not know that the real reason she wanted a front porch was so she would have an excuse to do more gardening! I know this was what my subconscious was aiming for all along. And to think, if my puppy hadn't dug the heck out of my lawn, it never would've happened!

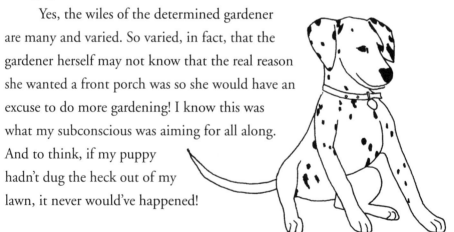

Catalog Inspiration

have a lot of gardening books. I've been a master gardener and a gardening columnist for a while, so naturally I pick up a lot of publications on the subject. But guess what I use more than anything else when I'm drawing up a landscape plan. My co-op extension file box? My Rodale organic gardening set? My *Sunset Western Garden Book*? Nope. I pick up my catalogs.

Catalogs? Those pulpy things that come in the mail? Yep. I send off for every seed, plant, and speciality gardening catalog I can find, and keep every last one. I have hundreds in boxes jammed in my closet. Most of them were free, and the rest cost a buck or two, but they are more valuable to me than all my books put together. And the great part is that once you've sent off for a few, a whole bunch more show up later thanks to mailing lists.

Some have pictures, all glossy and better looking than the plants themselves. I use those for my planning scrapbook. Just cut out pictures of all the plants you might like to have, including the helpful descriptions captioned underneath, and tape them to some paper. You can't do that to your expensive books. When you've got a hundred or so laid out, you can then go through and easily pick out those that require sun, those that require shade, those that bloom in spring, and those that bloom in fall to give yourself a balanced, long-blooming garden. And it's great fun, too, like when you made scrapbooks as a kid.

Some of these catalogs are thick, weighty tomes, better resembling a paperback Stephen King novel than a seed catalog, but catalogs they are, nonetheless, and useful, too. They have no pictures, but they offer something else to the discerning gardener: easy access to botanical names. Why do you need to know botanical names?

Well, let's say you're reading a stuffy gardening magazine, minding your own business, when you spot a photograph of an adorable, simply wonderful, plumy pink thing that you must have. You eagerly check the caption, only to find that it is called *Filipendula rubra*. You are outraged. As usual, the snobs who edit the rag can't be bothered to give you the common name.

You say to yourself, "Now what the heck is that?" Even your little local nursery hasn't heard of it. Then you look up *Filipendula rubra* in your dry, alphabetized, picture-less catalog. Oh! The common name for that stuff is queen-of-the-prairie! Trust me, queen-of-the-prairie is much easier to locate than *Filipendula rubra*.

But be careful when ordering from your catalogs. Many are quite on the up-and-up, but some are downright deceitful. I won't name names, but a certain company wows you with photos of stupendous perennials that literally make your mouth water. Then, about a month after you've ordered, the mailman brings you a sorry-looking paper sack filled with shriveled roots, tubers with only one eye, and bulbs that a gopher would turn up his nose at. You're lucky if they bloom in three years, let alone this year.

But on the whole, I love my catalogs. I usually order my bulbs from them because they're cheaper than the ones I can get locally, but mostly I use them for ideas to take with me on my next trip to the nursery. Of course, unless you live in a big city, it's hard to find some of the more unusual stuff down at Bobby Joe's Nursery and Hardware. In that case, order straight from the catalog by all means.

But first, you must go order some catalogs! Do it now! Their inspiration value alone is priceless.

Aesthetic Reasons Alone

Give yourself a plot for a perennial bed.
It doesn't have to be big, and it doesn't have to be fancy, but you really should do it. You should do it because a perennial bed doesn't provide you with nourishing food the way your vegetable garden does. You should do it because it does not provide you with cooling shade the way your trees do. You should do it because it does not provide a place for your children to play like your lawn does. In fact, it has no practical purpose whatsoever.

And that is exactly why you should do it.

Life is a big chore most of the time, with everything we do necessarily resulting in some worthwhile benefit to ourselves and our families. We work so we can pay the bills and keep a roof over our heads. We own cars and make big payments on them so we can get to work, mostly. We clean our homes so our families don't become dirty pigs, and so various bugs and germs don't get on us and make us sick.

Our yards are microcosms of our lives. Many believe, mistakenly, that everything in them must serve a purpose. The grass, the trees, the veggie patch. But in the macrocosm of life, do we not occasionally go on reviving vacations? Do we not read the Sunday comics? Do we not laugh at a TV sitcom or scream obscenities as our favorite football team fumbles the ball?

All these things are fun. They serve no purpose except to be fun, to cause fun, to encourage fun. Your yard needs some fun, too.

I know, I know, you have objections. Well, let me shoot those down right away. "I don't have time for a perennial bed." Horsepucky. You can dig it up in one Saturday. Measure out a sunny spot (I like to spray paint the outline on the grass), and dig it up. Throw in a couple bales of peat moss and some manure, and mix it up with your shovel. Later, your perennials will take care of themselves, since they never need to be replanted. The little suckers just keep coming back every year.

"I can't afford it." Bullroar. If you can't afford a $4.00 bale of peat moss, throw in your grass clippings. Or maybe your soil doesn't need anything. Or go to your closest large animal owner and offer to take some of his horse manure off his hands. You only need a couple of bags.

The cost of the perennials itself is not that bad. And don't worry about filling the bed up immediately. Besides, when the bed is dug, an amazing phenomenon takes place. Suddenly, everyone you know wants to give you a clump of whatever they've got because they have too much, or because of that trait gardeners are born with that makes them want to share the joy they've gotten out of a certain plant. I once filled an entire 20' x 5' perennial border that way. It was completely stuffed with offerings from neighbors, parents, and friends within two years. I know I actually bought one plant for it, but for the life of me I can't remember what it was. One of the loveliest traits of a perennial bed is that its inhabitants are usually extremely prolific. They just keep growing and spreading, necessitating the giving of excess to friends.

No, your perennial bed will not further your income, advance your career, or make your husband wash the dishes more often. But it will please your eye. It will gladden your soul. Your neighbors will believe you've got the heart of an artist, which you will, if you don't already, because gardening, like art, serves the grandest purpose of all.

It tells us, "Yes, we need to struggle to survive. But we are set apart from all the other creatures who must also struggle because we can create this and, furthermore, we can enjoy it!" The Merriam-Webster Dictionary defines aesthetics as "a branch of philosophy dealing with the nature, creation, and appreciation of beauty." So go. Go be an aesthete!

Manure, Lawn Clippings, & the Compost Elite

 et's talk about compost. I mean seriously, let's get real down and dirty here, folks, to turn a phrase.

A good many of you have some and don't know it. I'm speaking of the horse owners whose gigantic pile of forkings from old Blaze's stall make the mouths of rose gardeners water in raging envy every time they drive past. For those of you who are lucky enough to own a Blaze or a Flossie, your gardening fortunes are made. Horse manure is the greatest thing for your roses when shoveled right on top of the soil as a dressing. It won't hurt them. I know many people fear it will burn the roots, etc., but it won't. Just don't let it cram right up against the canes, and you'll be fine.

But if you're looking to make your manure pile good for all of your flowers, you've got to help it out a little. When your leaves drop next autumn, add those. When you mow the lawn, put your clippings in. Throw a little good vegetable garden dirt in for the worms, and put a little more on top of the pile. Water your pile every so often, too, because when it gets dry, the microbiotic decay processes halt, and mold and mildew begin to grow, causing clumping and all-around nasty smells. Turn it every couple of weeks for a month or so, and it's ready.

What? You don't have any manure to put on your pile? Well, some people think that adding their kitchen food scraps to a compost pile is the answer. Not me! I find that it draws rodents. Yuck. So we'll pass on that idea for now, shall we?

Your gardening center sells a box of stuff proclaiming itself to be a compost maker of some sort or another that you can sprinkle on your pile. Oh, it works all right. But brother, is it a rip-off! All it is is fertilizer (usually 10-10-10), like what you spread on your lawn, around your bulbs, or whatever. For heaven's sakes, don't pay their inflated prices. Any old fertilizer you've got left over in your garage or shed will do just as well. Got a little lawn fertilizer from last spring moldering in a sack out back? Same thing. So-called "evergreen food?" That works fine on your compost, too, because what manure and those dry, granulated fertilizers have in common is nitrogen, and a lot of it. And that's what your pile wants.

So, what do you put in your compost pile if you've never had one, don't know what to do, and don't know where to start? Everything you can find that is green or brown. A little dirt. You don't need a special box, or cage, or aerating tool. You don't need to buy compost maker. You don't need a gigantic drum that spins around at the flick of the wrist. All you need is a spot to pile stuff and a pitchfork. I've noticed that piles that fail generally do so because they weren't turned or watered enough. Otherwise, they work pretty fine.

Let's not be distracted by the compost elite, folks. It's no great, complicated secret. If it came from a living barnyard animal, throw it in. (No meat, fat, or dog or cat droppings, please). If it used to grow in your yard, throw it in. If it's in a sack labeled lawn fertilizer, throw it in. And when it's all black and soft and dirty-looking, throw it on your flower beds.

It's great stuff.

Daffodils & Coffee Cups

All week I'm stuck inside an office, helping out my husband, who is temporarily between secretaries. And of course, the weather is stunning.

I keep having to tuck in my lower lip. It's hard not to pout when, after a long dreary winter, old Sol decides to smile benignly down on you. Or rather down on where you should be, tucking some sweet alyssum among the tulips in the east bed. But of course, old Sol can't find me because I am sitting at a desk, filing strange memo thingies, typing envelopes on a machine that belongs on a space shuttle, and answering a phone with a lot of buttons.

I planted a bunch of daffodils outside my husband's office a couple of autumns ago. Their fat, curious noses peeped out of the soil by the front entrance in early January this year. By the beginning of February, they were in full leaf. By last week they were in full bud, just waiting for a couple more warm degrees before exploding open in vivid, sweet-scented coronas of gold.

Except that some guy in heavy boots stepped on half of them when he decided he'd save ten whole seconds by walking through the daffodils instead of around them.

I looked at them the other morning as I dragged my body and spirit, unaccustomed to leaving the house before 10:00 A.M., to my husband's office. It was so sad. The blooms had been just about to open, too. Now their long, graceful stems lay flat on the ground, their hooded blossoms quivering feebly in the dirt.

Yeah, yeah, I know daffodil blossoms don't quiver unless it's windy. But still, if you only knew what heart I take from seeing the daffodils every spring after a long dreary winter, you'd understand. Especially since I was to spend the next week or so away from my own daffodils during the daylight hours.

I gathered the daffodils, cutting their stems where they were bent or broken, and took them into the office. The office is like a bachelor pad; it has no vases to speak of, unless one counts the varied and old unwashed coffee mugs that dot the landscape, sticky on their bottoms from the alchemy of coffee, DairyMate, and sugar. I pry one loose with a pop and put the daffodils in it. They immediately fall out, long-stemmed and top-heavy as they are.

I spy a tall, cardboard latté cup, emblazoned with the Starbucks logo. Aha! These bachelors are not total barbarians, I deduce. I wrap the stems in paper towels, stuff them into the cup, and add water. Just right. They stand tall and hold a place of honor on my desk.

I drive home Friday afternoon, just as the sun is setting. Peering anxiously at my orchard, I can see that the crocus have all bloomed! Their blooms are closed up for the night, of course, as crocus will not open unless the sun is kissing their soft cheeks, but joy! Perhaps during the weekend they will reward me.

You may remember how I told of planting hundreds of bulbs directly in the grass in my orchard last December. I promised I'd tell you how they did. They did enchantingly. Countless daffodils are just beginning to open. Dozens of crocus. Scores of little snow iris. And soon, a hundred little blue and white muscari, their grape-like heads peeking out of the grass even as I speak. It is thrilling.

So I looked at that orchard a lot this weekend. Got my spring fix, you might say. And tomorrow I will trudge back to the office. But guess what. I only have another week to go, but all the same, my wonderful husband took pity on me, telling me he only needed me in the afternoons.

Believe you me, I plan on spending the next week's worth of mornings up to my knees in mulch, flats of sweet alyssum (which I will be tucking around the tulips in the east bed), and daffodils. Beautiful, beloved daffodils.

In the meantime, in the afternoons, I will look up from my twenty-first century office machinery and gaze at the splendid little fellows in the Starbucks cup. And that will be good enough.

JAK

The Daily Walking Tour

ith the arrival of spring, I've once again begun the daily walking tour of my garden. The walking tour is essential and pleasurable, and I never tire of my herbaceous wards, even after repeated viewings.

I began the walking tour many years ago with my very first garden, if one can call the grass I dug up under the peach tree and the small plot under my living room window a garden. I was twenty-five years old, new to the game, and unsure as to whether my plants would survive my uncertain skills. Under the peach tree I'd planted tall phlox, sweet william, hollyhocks, columbines, begonia tubers, and some annuals like marigolds, bushy sweet pea, and stock.

Under my window I put what I hoped were shade lovers: a bush variety fuchsia, a lot of impatiens, some monarda, and a bunch of lily-of-the-valley pips.

Anxiously, I surveyed these little tubers, roots, pips, and starts like a mother with a new baby, checking on them often. I think my neighbors thought I was odd, walking around my front yard six times a day, often kneeling and peering worriedly at the tiny things, hoping to see growth and health—hoping not to see aphids, whiteflies, and mildew. But I had spent $75.00 on those plants, a goodly sum, especially since I had recently given up my job to become a full-time homemaker and we were still in that painful transition between two incomes and one. My husband was not too thrilled at the expense, and I didn't want to compound the problem by watching that $75.00 wilt to the ground like, well, like dead plants.

The walking tour paid off on the very first day, when the marigolds began to droop not three hours after I'd planted them. The weather was warm and I, in my ignorance, had not watered them in when I planted them. I scowled at them, scratching my head, and consulted my husband, who at least had a small vegetable patch in the backyard, his first.

"Did you water them in?" he asked. I shook my head. "What? How could you not know that?" he asked, apparently expecting a neon "idiot" sign to start blinking on my forehead. I watered the marigolds, and they perked right up.

Thus was born the walking tour, which I have performed at least once each day in the eight intervening years, no matter what, between March and October. My garden is lucky to receive one walking tour a month during the rest of the year since I've never been one of those gardeners who has the heart to struggle with winter-blooming plants. By October I am tired of gardening. By January I possess a flickering desire to skim my nursery catalogs, and by February I am eagerly awaiting the arrival of the crocus, those clever little darlings that pop up without any demands or help. But I await them from my window mostly.

By March, my gardening circuit breakers have been manhandled into their full "On, by golly, on!" positions, and I am wandering happily on my regular route through the property. Aha! The red-fleshed peony stalks are a good inch taller since yesterday! Drat! The dog has dug up two Japanese iris bulbs! Ten roses are hopelessly blackened from that horrible freeze. The hyacinths are all up and unfurled; now they can spare a few of their scented number for the vase on my kitchen table. The plum tree blossoms are opening! What? An aphid already? Whew, I was afraid that special daylily had died, but there are the tips of its stubborn new shoots, unseen yesterday. Thank heavens.

And so I tour my garden, and it is never dull. For its dwellers, like any other creature, do something different every day, speaking to me of their joys and woes as clearly as I speak to them of my own.

By the way, you do know that you should talk to your plants, don't you? No? Well, you can do it while you're taking your walk with them.

They are exceedingly pleasant companions.

The Wood Man

oday I had myself a good laugh. There's no moral to this story, I just thought I'd share with you the special relationship I have with my wood man.

My wood man is supposed to bring us split seasoned cordwood once a year. He is a nice fellow; you'd like him. But he is, shall we say, not well organized.

Case in point: last September we called the wood man and requested a couple cords of wood. He graciously agreed to deliver it in two days' time, on Wednesday.

On Tuesday I received a phone call. "Hello, is your husband there?" a man asked. "No," I said, "but maybe I can help?" He replied, "I was just wondering if you guys wanted some wood this year." I responded, puzzled, "But we just talked to you yesterday and you said you'd deliver some tomorrow!" There was a pause while he digested that. "Oh," he said, "oh, that's right!" And we hung up.

The next day he didn't show. Phone calls on our part could not locate him. A week later he called and asked us if we still wanted some wood. He said that he had not made it the previous week because he had to see the dentist. I wondered silently how having dental work could render a person unable to pick up a phone.

"Well, not anymore," I said, explaining truthfully, "I'm afraid you lost your place in the money line for this month. Call us back in October if you still have some wood." October rolled by, then November. We called and called but could not reach him. Finally, on December first, he called.

"You guys want any wood?" he asked. "Yes!" said my husband, "bring it on!" By this time, we needed wood desperately, and could find no one else this late in the season who would part with any. We had actually wanted the wood two months previously. Again, the wood was scheduled to be delivered in two days' time. But the next day, I got another call. "You guys want some wood?" he asked. I gaped at the phone. "Yes!" I said. "You said you'd bring some tomorrow!" He said, "Oh, that's right!" And the next day, finally, we got our wood—a huge pile that would last for months. It was wet, but beggars can't be choosers.

JAK

Two days later I got a call. Yes, it was the wood man. "You guys need any wood?" he asked. The hairs on the back of my neck stood up. "You already brought it," I explained in measured tones, "the day before yesterday." We hung up amicably enough, though I muttered an eye-rolling expletive while wondering how much laughing gas the wood man's dentist had administered the previous September.

A week later, believe it or not, the wood man telephoned again. Once more he queried, in what seemed by now to be duncelike tones, whether we needed any wood. He had forgotten, once again, that he had already sold us some. Again I assured him, somewhat testily this time, that he had already delivered it.

And today, two and a half weeks after receiving said wood, I got another call. "Hey," said a familiar voice. I jumped back and stared at the receiver in my hand. "You guys need any wood?"

I'm ashamed to say that I started to laugh. Curiously, he asked what was the matter, but I was too busy telling my children what I was laughing about, and they were laughing, too. "Hey," he asked plaintively, "what's the deal?"

I finally choked out, "How many times are you going to call and ask me if I need any wood?"

"Why," he said in surprise, "just this once."

Making Beauty, *Not* Excuses

Many of us cannot afford grand gardening schemes. Vita Sackville-West, English gardener extraordinaire of the early twentieth century, may have been able to set up an awe-inspiring, bazillion-acre garden on her manor estate, but good old Vita didn't have to work for a living; plus, she had lots of green stuff. Sawbucks. Lettuce. Dough. Money. Currency of the English Realm.

She was rich.

Some of us only aspire to such financial heights. Our greatest scheme for getting rich is winning the lottery.

However, the lack of a large bank account is no excuse for abandoning the beautification of your home! Shame on you for even considering such a thing. Would you step out in public in your torn pj's and mud mask? Then why would you let your property face the public everyday without benefit of good grooming?

I'll give you some ideas, just to get you started.

If you have a medium- to large-size tree of any type on your property, why not hang some potted fuchsias from the branches, put a lawn chair and a little table under them, and place a few pots full of (shade-loving) impatiens, hostas, lady's mantles, Virginia bluebells, ferns, or bleeding hearts around the spot? Then you could sit there on a hot day, sipping your cool drink of choice, and patting yourself on the back for creating such a pleasant little nook.

Do you have a fence? Plant a climbing rose (at anywhere from $4.00 to $8.00 apiece) at its base, and drape its long canes over the fence when they're grown. Pick something fragrant like 'Zéphirine Drouhin,' a beautiful pink baby whose canes grow up to twelve feet long, or red 'Blaze,' which, although its masses of gorgeous blossoms have no scent, blooms continuously for months, and is virtually carefree. The 'Cécile Brunner' climber is next to foolproof, with hundreds of lovely, scented, old-fashioned flowers.

If you have a front porch of any type, sweep it off and, again, put some potted flowers on it, taking care that you don't place them where people walk and the screen door swings. This need not cost much. Fill any old pots (you can always paint ugly ones, and even old wooden boxes or any kind of container will look charming) with soil, sprinkle in some annual seeds of any type, and leave them in a sunny, out-of-sight location until they start to bloom. If you start your pots in early spring, they'll be blooming before summer.

Next fall, plant some daffodils or tulips in these pots, make sure they drain well outside somewhere all winter, and bring them to your porch when their flowers open. I've seen people plant flowers in all kinds of things, from old cooking pots with a hole punched in the bottom to the classic terra-cotta, and they all look nifty when their leafy charges are in full tuck. My favorite seed for potted beauty is the 'Supersnoop' sweet pea, which trails out of its container when not piling up in a riotous, glorious mountain of bloom. It doesn't climb, and it's impervious to black thumbs.

Attach some boxes under your windows and your house will be transformed into an old-fashioned cottage. Petunias and marigolds do especially well in window boxes, as they're grown easily from seeds sown directly into the soil.

If you have some cracks in your sidewalk, between pavers or bricks, or in a rock wall or rock garden, tuck in a few sprigs of Irish or Scotch moss. Moss forms soft little mounds that can be stepped on with impunity.

My children and I love to go barefoot over ours, wiggling our toes in its plush pile carpet. Moss also grows dear tiny flowers in the summer, adding a pretty green counterpoint to the browns and reds and grays of the earth, bricks, or stones that surround it.

If you have a small front yard and are sick of trying to keep the grass green during long summer droughts, kill the grass. You heard me right. Use Roundup or some other all-purpose plant killer. When it's dead, rake up the old stuff and get rid of it. After a couple weeks, plant some Irish moss, creeping thyme, and other ground-hugging herbs; roll it, water it, and otherwise tend it (at first) like you would a new lawn. Herbs prefer poor soil and dry conditions, so, once established, your herb lawn will rarely need feeding, mowing, or much watering. And yes, you can walk on it, although a game of touch football should probably be avoided.

JAK

Hang a potted *bougainvillea* or two from your porch rafters. Plant a Pink Dogwood (*Cornus florida* 'Rubra') in your front yard for elegant, sigh-inducing beauty. Plant a *Buddleia davidii,* or Butterfly Bush, and watch the butterflies come by the dozen. Plant a yellow Trumpet Vine *(Campsis radicans* 'Flava'*)* next to a window, and train the vine to climb up and around it. The vine does not need to be fastened in any way.

The possibilities are not just endless, they're exquisite. Divine. Gorgeous. Dazzling. Ravishing. Resplendent.

They're beautiful.

Rich People's Gardens

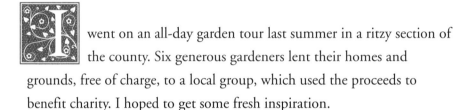went on an all-day garden tour last summer in a ritzy section of the county. Six generous gardeners lent their homes and grounds, free of charge, to a local group, which used the proceeds to benefit charity. I hoped to get some fresh inspiration.

The lead-in garden was a stunner. Surrounding a brick country mansion on ten acres, it was the paragon of every gardener's dream. A lush herb garden flowed around the house on two sides. A gigantic vegetable garden with gigantic vegetables was laid out in a massive grid pattern, with soft, thick straw laid down between each row. Raised beds encircled by evenly sized river stones contained tomato plants heavy with fruit. Nearby, an enclosed berry patch sent the children into ecstasy with its "eat all you can pick" policy.

A rare, dwarf apple orchard graced a half acre all by itself. Perennial beds, like oases of rainbow essence, were everywhere. Everything was lush and perfect. Nearly every inch of five acres was covered with splendid growing stuff, perfectly mulched, trimmed, edged, and cared for. A horse barn nearby provided brown gold. After my initial attack of wonder at the beauty of the place, I felt curiously disheartened. How could I possibly create or manage a garden this big? This perfect? This healthy? I found out from a docent whose name tag proclaimed her to be Agatha that the family had a full-time gardener. Ah.

The next home gave my heart a lift. It was an old farmhouse, like mine, surrounded by a small, city-lot-size cottage garden. Fabulous! Something I could handle! I marvelled at the collection of old-fashioned roses on the south side of the house. A postage stamp front yard, green as Ireland, was framed by a semi-circular bed of tall hollyhocks, daisies, miniature roses, and the like. A gate with an arch was pleasant to pass through; the sweet smelling rose and clematis that climbed over it dripped next to one's hair. But everything was so perfect. There was so very much mature, perfect plant material. I approached another docent, who sat next to a table covered with papers.

"Excuse me," I said. She immediately launched into an oft-repeated speech, handing me a large photocopy of a professional landscape blueprint. "This lovely garden," she droned, "was designed and implemented by Joe Blow and Associates of Bainbridge Island last year." Last year? But, it would take me ten years, at least, to grow a garden like that. I looked at the blueprint. Thousands of little squiggly circles, depicting plants, were laid out in an apparently random fashion. Instant garden. Oh, well, it was a beautiful thing anyway. Maybe I could do that at my house. Given ten years.

The third garden belonged to an ultra-modern house, the entire east wall of which overlooked Puget Sound and Seattle across the water. The

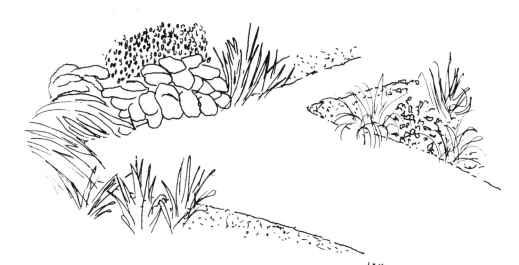

JAK

house was nestled in a cool acre of forest, and the garden was one designed
for shade and humidity. Hostas, conifers, trillium, and more crept seemingly naturally among the cedars and Douglas firs. Exotic ferns abounded.
A tiny man-made creek wound its way through it all. We followed a path
and were warned not to venture off it. After shuffling single file through
the beautifully landscaped woods for a while, we came out next to the
homeowner's tennis court. Tennis court? Water view? Wait a minute. There
was a little sign. It said "Landscaping designed and maintained by John
Doe and Associates."

Didn't any of these people actually garden? My nose was out of joint,
but the next home on the tour seemed different. It had the look, although
large and unusual, of a garden that was cared for by a real home gardener.
Funny little statues and birdfeeders dotted the landscape. The paths were
rough and covered in sawdust. Cool, I thought. Enthusiastic gardeners
must live here. It wasn't perfect enough. But it was great.

Enthusiastic gardeners did live there. One was a landscape designer.
One was a landscape artist. Hmph. So much for gardening for the common man.

I was not sure if I wanted to see the next two gardens. My own dear
little garden became shabbier and shabbier in my mind with each home I
visited. After all, so far the only inspiration these gardens had given any of
us was the inspiration to get rich, and nobody needs to see some gardens to
want that. But I had paid my money, and was determined to see it
through. Finally, we came to the last garden. I got out of my car, trudged
listlessly up a dirt road, and came around a corner of trees. The view that
awaited me made me laugh with relief. The garden looked just like mine!
A moldy but charming old apple orchard hovered over some odds and
ends lawn furniture. The vegetable garden was a hodgepodge of this and
that. A homemade greenhouse protected some seedlings. This I had to see.
I really wanted an affordable greenhouse. It was great. Flowers sprung up
here and there around the house, wherever someone decided they needed a

space for that flat of pansies or box of bulbs they had just brought home. I was interested in their novel, homemade watering system. The owners themselves wandered around, explaining how they'd done it all. A few people wandered to their cars, disinterested after seeing the glories of the other fancier gardens. Not me. This was a real garden, an achievable garden, with some new ideas I hadn't thought of that I could actually try for myself.

I went home happy. Still, I did try to line my vegetable garden with straw like the lords of the manor at the first stop did. Well, what a crock. The straw, full of straw seeds, sprouted immediately and drowned out the vegetables in a matter of weeks.

Shade Gardens & Yard Junk

ucked into the north side of my house was this annoying little corner. It sat on the shady side of my tall cement back porch steps, next to the rhododendron bed, and hardly got any sun at all. Grass and weeds grew listlessly under a water spigot, and the area had become a popular catchall for hoses, rakes, various sports equipment, a pair of my gardening gloves (which had been tied to jute twine by my industrious boys and hung from the porch railing, I have no idea why), a rusting barbecue grill, and several half-chewed dog toys.

I gave up trying to keep the area cleared out. Like Bethlehem, it drew more pilgrims every day. What to do? It was an eyesore. I looked around my yard, noticing that the flower beds were generally clear of such family debris, save for the occasional basketball or trowel.

After seconds of deep, brilliant, deductive thought, I came to a stunning conclusion. Grass = junk. Flower beds = flowers. Aha!

I threw the offending refuse over my shoulder with abandon. This was difficult to do with the barbecue, but I persevered. My mission, should I choose to accept it: A Shade Garden. A little one, for sure. The area was only about fifty square feet.

Sighing heavily, I hunted for my spade. Oh, how I hated this part of gardening. Digging up sod for a new bed is extremely hard on one's back. Nevertheless, I stiffened my upper lip, dug up about nine square feet and then did what I always do. I begged my husband with piteous, heartbreaking pleas until he stomped out in exasperation and finished the work in about two minutes. Honestly, I don't know why it's so hard to get him to do this; it's so easy for him. The same work would've taken me all week. But you see, I've got this old football injury.

Time for the fun part. That's where I tell him to get lost, and I take over the creation of the flower bed. He becomes strangely absent from any and all future accounts I give to people of how I made the bed. I, of course, did it all single-handedly. My husband understands and respects this attitude. Perhaps it isn't macho to admit to helping your wife make a flower bed, although I don't know why. I've known many macho gardeners. Some of them were even men.

The junk was gone, the sod was gone. I realized I must replace the missing stuff with better stuff. I dumped horse manure, compost, and peat moss in my heavy soil, tossing them together with the dirt like a chef's salad. I could've double-dug, but the area was small, the earth was fairly loose and easy to dig, and besides, I didn't want to.

Fluffy and friable, my soil now awaits its new inhabitants. I make a list of plants that like living in partial to full shade. I'll try some Wedding Phlox (*P. maculata*) to see if it can stand only an hour or so a day of sun. I'll even try some flag iris; I've had good luck with that before in dimly lit areas. I know that yellow corydalis will do well here as it is a cousin of bleeding heart, which does well in this kind of light, and I add them both to my list. What else? Can't do without astilbe. Red ones, I think. A daylily might bloom here—I'll stick one in just to see. Bellflowers. Definitely a big hosta in the corner to hide the spigot. Some gloxinia, Geranium (*G. ibericum platypetalum*), ooh, and a big clump of lady's mantles, with their dear little masses of lemon yellow flowerlets. Do I have room for more? Hmmm, as usual, fifty square feet is more space than one expects it to be.

Of course, I could stop right there, and the plants already mentioned would fill the bed within a couple of years on their own. But this time I don't feel like waiting a couple of years. Lily-of-the-valley it is then, around the edges. Virginia bluebells. Honey-scented yellow violas. And I've always meant to try a cinnamon fern, so I'll put one near the back. I call the nursery and demand a rush delivery.

Packages of roots, tubers, and seedlings arrive a couple of weeks later, after my soil has rested a little. I throw my schedule to the wind and devote the day to tucking them into their new bed. No slapdash work here; this part is important. I lay the plants around the bed until I've got them where I want them. I scoop back a little soil, lovingly laying the bottom of a plant in and backfilling a bit. With a watering can full of plant food-tainted water, I spill some into each basin. I let it sink in. I fill the rest of the hole up with soil, tamp it lightly, and move on to the next.

Finished. I now await May, the month when March's efforts start coming into glory. My dark little corner will be bright at last.

But I still don't know what I'm going to do with all the junk that used to be there.

Offerings & Thievery

am emotionally drawn to memories of my last garden, that small subdivision lot in town. I miss it partly because it was my first serious garden, but mostly because of what I left behind.

Most of the plants in those small front and back yards were given to me by other gardeners, or by non-gardeners who didn't want the sad, bareroot offerings they had tugged out of their properties. A neighbor gave me several clumps of Heartleaf (*Bergenia cordifolia),* a low-growing perennial with large, thick leaves and tall, slender stalks topped by clusters of sweet, pale lavender flowers that bloomed early in the spring with the first tulips. This same neighbor shared her wild, dark blue Columbine (*Aquilegia alpina*) with its fairy heads that nod in the breeze, as well as a good clump each of her shrubby flowering almond and forsythia.

The man who owned the lot that backed up against my backyard was hunched over his foundation border one day, not long after I moved in. He was tossing piles and piles of greenery over his shoulder and swearing. I wistfully latched my fingers through the chain link that separated us and asked him what the stuff was.

"Don't know," he said sparingly. "Too much of it. Don't want it. Gonna burn it." I squeaked "no" and asked if I could have it. Obligingly, he threw it all over the fence to me. I inspected the long, floppy blades and massive root systems, and, although I was a novice, decided I had some exceedingly healthy and unknown daylilies before me, piles of them.

I spent the whole day planting them, and was rewarded the following spring by more yellow blooms than I could count. Unlike any daylily I'd ever seen, these had an extremely strong, heady scent, and they spread like wildfire. That was fine by me. I liked fast spreaders because I couldn't afford to buy many plants with actual money. I adored those daylilies, and still don't know what variety they are. The only other place I've seen them is in an antique garden in front of an old Victorian mansion we visited once.

My father gave me a quince start, a few big clumps of old-fashioned, spicy-smelling pinks, and baby azaleas that he had tenderly rooted off his own monsters. A friend showed up one day with a large box of sad, bareroot roses. She said, "A friend of mine's mother-in-law pruned these one day while my friend was on vacation, and it made her mad because she doesn't like her mother-in-law. Out of spite, she pulled them all up and was fixing to put them in the burn barrel. I thought you might like to have them." Would I! One of them, a grand old 'Cécile Brunner' climber, I brought with me to my current house, where it covers my ugly, tall, concrete back porch wall like a gift from above. The list goes on and on.

We eventually outgrew the little house. On moving day, I decided I would supervise my moving men in unloading my furniture, then head back to the old place to take little starts from many of these plants. I couldn't dig them all up and leave the landscape bare after having sold the place partly because of the beauty of the gardens. But the new owners appeared while we were cleaning up, and refused to budge. They followed us around the house while we vacuumed and collected odds and ends, suspicious that we might steal something! My husband looked at me, I looked at him, and we started to leave. "What about the lawn?" the woman screeched. "What about that pile of compost? What about that huge pile of rose trimmings? Aren't you going to clean it up for us?"

"Do it yourself," I said angrily. Impulsively, I got a shovel out of my truck and headed for the backyard. That's when I dug up the 'Cécile

Brunner.' The harpy started to harangue me, but I said, "This does not belong to you," and she shut up. We left everything else behind.

Well, except for one other thing. Two weeks later I lay sleepless once again in my bed at 2:00 A.M. grinding my teeth over the woman's attitude and my lost lovelies. What bothered me most was not getting a clump, not even a piece, of those old, scented daylilies. I knew I'd never find them in a catalog or a nursery again. The neighbor who had given them to me had moved. I made a decision and leapt out of bed.

I drove over to my old house in the dead of night, dressed in black and feeling dangerous. I parked right in front, got out my shovel, and, under the bright streetlight that shines on my old yard, dug up a gigantic clump of my daylilies. I did not try to be quiet. The patron saints of fools and gardeners must have been smiling on me. I slammed my car door with my dirt-laden booty beside me and roared off unchallenged.

Now those daylilies spread their roots all around the base of the 'Cécile Brunner,' and I don't feel a bit guilty.

JAK

On Chores, Babies, & Ladders

hen I was a child, I didn't "get" gardening for pleasure. To me it meant weeding the carrots, pulling rocks out of the pasture, digging up potatoes and hauling them to the big bins in the cool pump house, digging dandelions out of the lawn with a butter knife for a penny apiece, and holding the ladder for Dad while he stood atop it, pruning the alders by the road so that the power company wouldn't butcher them.

Gardening was work, plain and simple. It was what I did to make sure that: the carrots grew big; the pony didn't break his leg; the potatoes didn't rot in the ground; the lawn stayed healthy; and my father didn't fall ten feet and break his back for a third time. It was what had to be done before I could go riding or swimming in the creek. It had to be done before I could curl up on my bed and read a Walter Farley book. Ah, yes, *The Black Stallion*, *The Island Stallion*, *The Blood Bay Colt*, the stuff that little girls' dreams are made of.

Gardening was an annoyance that interfered with what I really wanted to do.

The mind works in mysterious ways. For as long as I can remember, people have told me that I am just like my father. We are both a little brash at times. We put our feet in our mouths as if they were chocolate chip cookies. We have a weakness for helpless people, animals, and babies, that we don't like others to see.

I admired my father greatly. Still do. I think that I wanted to be like him. He raised animals of all sorts for our income and consumption, so the things that held the most fascination for me as a child were animals. When we girls grew up, he converted the farm into a garden, so I don't think it's a coincidence that my intense affections switched about that time from animals to gardening. I didn't realize it then, but at the age of twenty-three I was still trying to be like my father. Gardening was my way of forming a special bond with him that no one else in my family shared. It may be true that I was subconsciously aping him, but that is not the reason I continued to garden. My interest in it grew into something far beyond maintaining a bond with a parent.

Gardening became a pure pleasure, and that amazed me. But, gardening is work! A chore! How could it be so much fun?

Once again, one of my father's penchants had become my own. I love babies, but there are only so many babies a person can reasonably have. After realizing that I couldn't have babies around the house for the rest of my life, I required an alternative supply of sweet, helpless things to care for. Puppies, kittens, birds—they fill that niche fairly well, but there's a limit to how many of those you can have as well. And then I discovered gardening for pleasure.

You can never have too many baby plants! There they are, all wee and darling, requiring your aid and succor to survive. You can watch them grow from infancy to youth, from youth to adolescence and maturity, and when they're grown you can always dig up another little bed and plant more babies. There are, of course, a finite number of plants one can stuff into any piece of property. But according to Teresa's Theory of Unlimited Space, you

JAK

could conceivably continue to add more plants to your property forever, so long as you don't plant every square inch all at once. After all, plants die, making way for new ones. Cold snaps take them, or windstorms, or neighborhood thieves. Dogs dig them up, cats defile them, aphids defoliate them, or you forget to water them when it's hot outside. Sure, gardeners always moan about how difficult it is to protect their gardens from all the disasters that await them, but gardeners are secretly glad when a mole eats every last tulip in the south bed. They can go buy some more now, you see, and feel perfectly justified.

Now I believe I've come full circle. I no longer separate the "chore" part of gardening from the "fun" part. It's all fun: the mowing and the pruning of trees and the weeding of carrots and the popping of dandelions. I asked my son to hold my ladder for me recently while I climbed atop it to reach a cedar branch that the wind had snapped. It hadn't broken all the way through, and hung dangerously over the road where my neighbors regularly stroll. I had to stand on the very top of the ladder to reach it with my clippers, putting way too much trust in my twelve-year-old son. As I reached my arms high, the ladder wobbled dangerously. Just in time, I remembered what happened the last time I held the ladder for my father's pruning efforts, when I was also twelve. It started to wobble, I couldn't keep it from falling, and Dad fell. It traumatized me severely, though he managed to escape unscathed.

I climbed down the ladder, sent my boy off to play, climbed the tree itself, and thoroughly enjoyed the chore of cutting off that branch.

Absence & Homecoming

y husband and children and I just returned from a four-day trip to Oregon, trusting that not much could change in such a short time span. I should have known better, for it is always while one is away that one's garden decides either to accept every disease and pest that shows its face, or to transform itself into a wondrous thing of beauty.

Happily, this time the latter took place.

My tulip bed, with its fading hyacinths, possessed many leafy tulip greens five days ago, and yes, many buds. But the buds were closed tight against the rain and wind, and were yet green. When we returned, they were nearly unrecognizable, and if I had not had a clear memory of having planted them last fall, I would've thought that some dear Tulip Fairy had deposited the scores of brightly colored gems in my bed. How quickly they unfurled their reds and yellows, lavenders and pinks! The sun must have shone on them while I breathed the dry, clear air of the high Central Oregon Plateau.

The large, early 'King Alfred' daffodils crumpled into tired, golden wads while I was gone, yet the gentle colors of the next wave, smaller whites, bi-colors, and faded lemon and pastel shades had taken over in a burst of exuberance. I wandered through the orchard in awe. I had merely tucked them beneath the thick sod last fall. How did they manage to do all this?

The orchard. Before I left, only the plum trees had bloomed in their cloudy, white way. Now, they are joined by the 'King,' the 'McIntosh,' and the 'Transparent,' the apple trees' shades of pink bowing tenderly over their daffodil wards. White Muscari (*M. alba*) finally burst into bloom under the white-flowered plums, and the already swelling blue ones swelled even further, their chubby little blooms adding an air of unbearable cuteness to the scene.

The lilacs, covered a mere four days ago with small, hard, dark purple clusters of unopened bloom, decided to spread their wings while I wasn't looking, releasing their unique fragrance for nobody but my cats to sniff. Fortunately, their blooms last for several weeks, and my husband brought a large pitcher of them up to my office at the top of the house, as he does every year. I am compelled to hunt for some lilac perfume to wear on my wrists.

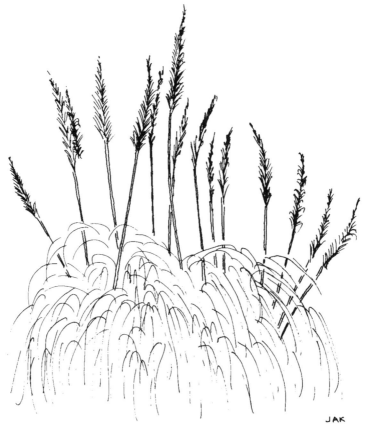

JAK

The clump of pampas grass near the driveway stills the worry I had carried in my heart. Last weekend, instead of cutting the old, yellowed growth down with a chain saw like I do every spring, I took a friend's advice and burned it down, knowing in my mind that the roots, energized, will send up even more fresh green shoots. But in my heart I was mortified. The blackened stubs frightened me. Surely I hadn't killed my lovely pampas?   No, I had not. Fresh green shoots did indeed greet us as we pulled up to our house after our long journey. I relaxed.

Did my flowers take heart from my absence, crying out to one another, "She's gone, we're free!" or rather, "Let's surprise her when she gets back?" I like to think that the latter is so. In the seventeenth century, Thomas Overbury wrote in *Newes of My Morning Worke:* "Absence doth sharpen love, presence strengthens it; the one brings fuel, the other blowes it till it burnes cleare." Oh happy thought, that little deception I allow myself: that my flowers' love for me sharpens while I'm gone, and strengthens when I return.

Or is it my love for them that brings the fuel? Both, I think.

Potting Sheds & Trenches

We have a small outbuilding right next to the vegetable garden. It's only about 6' x 6', but it has an adorable peaked cedar roof like our house, clapboard siding, a cupboard, a sink, and two windows. It used to be the creamery shed when our half-acre was the homestead of a one-hundred-acre dairy farm.

Soon, it will be my potting shed.

Right now, it's dirty and full of old plastic pots and yellowed newspapers. One cannot walk through it without climbing over junk. Spiders reign. The faucet on the sink has been turned around and shoved through a hole in the wall so that a hose could be run from it to the garden. One inside wall is covered with warped blue plywood.

However, I have a cunning plan.

It started innocently enough. A pile of rusted metal parts and other junk was leaning against one wall of the shed when I bought the place a year and a half ago. After I hauled it away, I was left with a gigantic bare spot. Since that wall had the morning and part of the afternoon sun, and since I would not need to strain myself by digging up grassy sod, I naturally decided to plant some flowers there. I was busy with other frightful finds around the property, so I took the path of least resistance and jammed a few lily bulbs in the dirt. I then sprinkled a bunch of oriental poppy seeds around them, and forgot about it, hoping it would take care of itself.

And how! The bright orange lilies and the daring red poppies brightened up that old shed like nobody's business last summer. Inspired, I went to clear out the winter weeds and sow some more poppy seeds yesterday. Hmm, I thought, the grass has encroached way too far this past year. Shouldn't I border the bed in a little and save myself some work next year? After all, it took me nearly three hours just to clear out a tiny 6' x 3' bed. I considered the usual options—adding dirt and raising the bed, surrounding it with rocks, using a railroad tie—and balked. I'd tried all those things in the past, and they just didn't look that great.

Then I remembered seeing a really fabulous garden last summer. The owner had trenched his beds. A lot of work, but this was such a small bed. I used my spade to cut a straight wall about six inches deep around the bed, allowing the soil to round back up the slope to the bed itself. By cutting this moat around the bed, making sure its bottom was below the level of the grass' roots, I effectively blocked the roots from wandering back into my poppies. When I finished, I stood back and looked at the site. Why, it looked beautiful! Easily the most attractive edging method I had ever used! Say, what if I made trenched beds all the way around my little shed?

And what if I gave it a new coat of paint? Yeah! And how about if I clear out the junk inside, hang up a rack for my gardening tools, paint everything in bright greens and yellows, and use it for a potting shed? Yeah! I'll tear off that old plywood. Absolutely! I'll wheedle my husband into repairing the plumbing, and since there's no electricity, I'll hang a Coleman lantern in there for those dusky summer nights when I have a hankering to sit in my cozy little potting shed and play in the dirt! Yeah!

JAK

My mind was awhirl with the cuteness quotient of my little shed. I'd hit the farmers' market and flea markets and bring home some inexpensive (but cute) things to hang on the walls inside. I'd build bins for potting soil, potatoes, fertilizers! I'd hang a little sign outside saying, "Keep Out, This Means You" to warn off my offspring, who would use it for a fort, or my husband, who would decide to clean engine parts on its counters.

I told all this to my husband, who shook his head sadly, obviously expecting a huge spending spree. But he's wrong. Wrong, I tell you! I have a million half-full cans of paint left over from the house. Shovel power is free. So is husband power. We already have a Coleman lantern, which I will usurp. I'll cannibalize my other flower beds for starts for the potting shed borders. The bins I will build from the old pile of lumber behind the garage. I am nothing if not resourceful. I'll wager that my potting shed transformation will cost under fifty bucks. After all, did I not once transform a nasty little back patio into a thing of beauty for $14.40?

So that's my project this week. Oh, the beds won't get made and the laundry won't get done; my novel will not get that fifteenth chapter it so badly needs, but what the heck. It's spring! The sun is shining! The adventures of gardening and renewal beckon!

Besides, I never make beds anyhow.

Observations *from an* Obsessed Gardener

At the beauty parlor today, I viewed dozens of hair swatches, trying to choose one shade of blond that I could live with for a while. I found myself drawn, again and again, to a lovely color known as champagne. After my stylist worked her magic, I happily took my new look home, only to discover, to my astonishment, the subliminal force that had drawn me to that particular shade: the dozens of pale, creamy yellow Darwin tulips swaying in the spring breeze next to my garage. Coincidence? I think not.

I went to the grocery store for a few dinner items last week. Diabolically, the store manager had placed a gigantic rack of seeds smack-dab in front of the entrance. I tried to pass them up, but doubled back, just for one packet of zinnias. The zinnia seeds looked so lonely in my empty cart that I threw in packets of sweet pea and cosmos to boot. Still other colorful packets beckoned. And they were only 99¢ cents apiece! What harm could one do at 99¢ per packet? After glancing furtively around, afraid that somehow my husband had unhooked himself from the baseball game and followed me to the store, I began throwing seed packets into my cart in a frenzied celebration of 99 centism. Of course, at the checkout stand I discovered that I had actually bought $25.00 worth of seeds and was suitably outraged. The bored cashier yawned and said, "So put them back," but of course I did not. That was the priciest 99¢ I've ever spent.

My favorite catalog company called me last spring, offering me the "biggest, fattest, best lily bulbs you'll ever see!" Usually happy with their goods, I eagerly ordered two dozen. When they came, they didn't look any bigger or fatter than any other lily bulbs in existence, but I planted them, hoping that the size would actually be in the plant itself. Come summer, those bulbs produced the smallest, spindliest, sickliest lilies in creation. Yesterday, that selfsame catalog company called me again, once more offering me those paragons of the lily world. I refused, and proceeded to chastise the man for last year's bulbs, describing in intricate detail the massive fault I found, and accusing the company of being ignorant of the phrase, "truth in advertising." After a long silence, the fellow finally said, "Hey, lady, I don't know anything about these #%@& plants," and hung up on me. You live and learn.

My husband is in a snit because I spent thirty bucks on some small gardening tools. It is a lovely set, solid stainless steel, one-piece construction, with a canvas gardening belt to carry them around in and the best weed popper I have ever used. "But I can buy you a hand trowel for 99¢ at the garden center," he complained. (There's that 99¢ again.) "You're missing the point," I replied, holding my dear little silver trowel close to my bosom. "These will last forever." He scowled at me. "Yeah," he retorted, "but for thirty bucks I can buy you new tools every year for seven years." I shrugged. If he couldn't see the long-term savings my lovely little set would bring about, there was nothing I could do about it. Fortunately, he didn't remember that I lose all of my tools, every year.

While bagging lawn clippings and dumping them on the compost heap last week, I threw my back out and was bedridden with terrible sciatica pain for three days. What genius can figure out why I dug up the perennial border around my potting shed on the fourth day, risking another lay-up and three more days of housework for my husband? What possesses me?

Speaking of backs, a writer friend of mine, who also happens to be a gardener, told me, "I have decided to give up gardening. My back, like a surgeon's hands, is a delicate instrument. I must save it for the long, grueling hours I spend slumped over my keyboard." I hear ya, babe! After a day's gardening, sitting at the computer is the back-pain equivalent of giving birth. To twins. At the same time.

Yet despite the pain, the frantic spring nursery sprees, a disgruntled husband, and hair the color of tulips, I cannot give up my gardening. To do so would go totally against my nature, Mother Nature, and unnatural hair color. Besides, everyone knows me as "Teresa Keene, that gardener chick." If I quit, what would everyone call me? "Teresa Keene, that chick who used to garden, but now sits in front of her computer every day, totally out of touch with reality?" Uuuugh. Makes me shudder.

JAK

Spontaneous, Herbaceous, Regenerative Restoration

All right, so I decided to have a little fun with you when I chose this chapter's title. But when we bought our old farmhouse, with its half-acre of equally old landscaping, confusion reigned over what to do with the trees. I had always told myself that if I ever had some grand old trees and shrubs, I would never hack them down and prune them silly, as I've seen so many homeowners do. I, with my pure gardener's heart and clever gardener's hands, would somehow jolly the things into submission with a gentle touch.

But since, as La Rochefoucauld said on the subject of egotism, "We would rather speak ill of ourselves, than not talk of ourselves at all," I must admit that the restoration of my old trees had almost nothing to do with my clever gardener's hands.

Take the holly trees, for example. As tall as my three-story house, they were hopelessly overgrown and their top two-thirds were spindly, unbalanced, and blighted. After ruminating for many months on various treatments, I wound up having a tree guy come out, lop the top two-thirds off, and shape the bottom third of each into a bell-shaped topiary. Ahhh, they're grand. But not cured by my clever hands.

And take the two gigantic western arborvitae-style cedars that flank my front gate. One could not pass through the gate when we moved in because the cedars had grown so wide that they had actually grown together. Also, they were yellowing badly from I knew not what. I did a hatchet job on the lowest seven feet of growth so that we could reach the gate, but that was all. After glumly chastising myself for many months, I can now safely say I must have inadvertently done something right, for the yellow is gone from their fronds and the tall, columnar trees look healthy and happy.

The gigantic old dogwood in the corner of my yard was dying. Our first spring in our happy home found me staring out the window at anthracnose, that insidious, wasting disease that native dogwoods are so susceptible to. The dogwood's leaves dropped as soon as they matured, dry and nastily curled. There was no April display of bright yellow blossoms. All summer the tree strove valiantly, producing new leaves over and over again, only to have the disease shrivel them up and push them off. I think of anthracnose as the Simon Legree of the tree world.

I was so busy with everything else that I didn't get around to spraying the poor tree. And there were so many other things around the house demanding our money that I couldn't justify hiring anyone to take care of it. I decided to take the easy route and simply cut it down later.

I don't know what happened—maybe the tree sensed my murderous intentions—but over the winter it somehow managed to shake off the anthracnose. April came, and just as I was eyeing my chain saw, the dogwood burst into full, glorious leaf. Warily, I waited for the leaves to drop, but they did not. Instead, a full shawl of the flat, lemony blossoms appeared, their primitive, four-petal selves gladdening my heart. The tree has not one trace of anthracnose. Another tree mysteriously not cured by my clever hands. I am nevertheless grateful.

Then there's the orchard, its fruit-bearing trees covered with a hairy hide of moss. The tree man who pruned the elderly suckers off the top told me to spray them with dormant oil to kill the moss. Apparently, the moss was killing the old trees. No, I said, enough is enough. I could not invest paycheck after paycheck into the trees. I could see a pattern materializing: all of the trees would grow sicker and sicker, and I would pay a fortune trying to save the geriatric things. Then they would fall down in a couple of years just the same. Just prune them, I told him, and we'll see what happens.

What happened was that the removal of the suckers let more sunlight into the orchard, and sunlight is the enemy of moss. This spring, the moss is decreased by half, drying out and flaking off so slowly that I didn't notice until recently.

So there you have it. Against my earlier vows, I did wind up pruning things silly, and not particularly cleverly. Most of the time, I had someone else come in and hack at my trees. Often, I did nothing at all when seasoned plantsmen were urging me to spray, spray, spray. Yet somehow, some way, my trees have mysteriously sprung back to life. Except for pruning the suckers off the apple trees, I've done almost everything wrong, according to the experts, anyway.

Perhaps the trees responded more to my pure gardener's heart than to my clever gardener's hands.

After *the* Party's Over

hey flop drunkenly, sheepishly, all around my house, almost as if they feel foolish for their earlier revelries. They bend their heads down as if to hold them in their hands, but, pitiably, their arms droop too badly to do any good, and their heads merely fall off, bit by bit. They'd like to lie down and rest, but their legs won't let them. They are quite forlorn.

My hyacinths, tulips, and daffodils—the jolly partakers of the powdery bulb food I put in their holes last fall—bloomed with a fervor unmatched by any bulbs I have ever planted before. But alas, I fear they imbibed too deeply, and if they were people, I would feel compelled to take away their car keys and make them sleep on my sofa.

So they had a wonderful time, and now they're sorry. So am I. Now I have a large area covered in limp, lazy green stalks and leaves, and I am helpless to mow or cut them down. After all, one must leave the leaves in place until they turn thoroughly brown, else the bulbs will not bloom well next year. They soak up nourishment in the form of sunlight, you see, fattening the bulb for another party three seasons hence. However, they are not attractive in the interim, not attractive at all. What to do?

First, you must go and pull out all the grass and weeds that have sprung up amongst them. Then, you should cut off the flowers' long stalks, being careful not to cut any green leaves. Finally, you need to stake all of the leaves down to the dirt with bent toothpicks.

This is not as strange as it sounds. Take your aging daffodil, for instance, and gently lay its leaves down onto the ground in a starburst pattern around the center of the plant. Bend a toothpick so that it forms an "L," and drive it through a leaf and into the dirt. The bent part of the toothpick will hold the leaf down. Please remember never to walk barefoot over this bed! When you're done, you will have leaves overlapping each other all over your bed, and it will look odd, but don't worry. The next step will take care of that.

Go and buy a couple of flats of young perennials or annuals, and tuck them into the dirt between the leaves. As they grow, the yellowing eyesores of that fabulous spring party will quickly be hidden. Just leave the yellowing leaves in place as a sort of self-mulch, for they will decay completely before summer's out. They'll keep the soil cool, you see, around the feet of your little additions, and that's a very good thing.

Just don't get impatient and careless and mow down all those sorry-looking leaves. I know what one thinks during every good party: "I hope this never ends!" But I also know what one thinks when one is holding one's head after every good party: "I am never doing this again!" Tut, tut, tut. It's like childbirth. You always forget the pain. And believe me, next spring, when you're about to tear your hair out from looking at your drab, endless, winter landscape, you will seriously look forward to the next grand party. Again, the hyacinths, daffodils, and tulips will revel and make you laugh. And don't worry about the hangover. Getting intoxicated from the beauty of this party will do you no lasting harm.

JAK

A Most Satisfactory Husband

y husband and I sit on resin lawn chairs still damp with rain in our orchard. "Look at that house," I say, pointing at our very own home. "It needs painting!" The paint—drab shades of blue and yellow—is chipped and worn. It does not do justice to the yard, I fear.

"Yes," my husband says, nodding. "We'll paint it this summer." I smile. I have a most satisfactory husband.

"And look," I say, "just look at that wonderful vista through the yard there, with all those wonderful old shrubs and trees. But the view is spoiled!"

"Spoiled?"

"Spoiled by that terrible chicken wire and stake fence our predecessors put around the yard! Can't we have a nice picket fence?"

"It looks rustic," he muses, stroking his beard.

"It looks like a turkey pen," I argue. "I'll help. I'll dig the post holes."

"Okay," he says agreeably. "This summer."

"The orchard looks nice," I say after a time. We sip our beer companionably.

"Yeah," he says, looking around. "Good thing I sprayed. If I'd waited till summer . . ."

"The bugs would've eaten them up," I finish. He nods. "Thanks for doing that," I add. He nods.

Dogs play in the grass beside us. The little one bites the big one's ankle until the big one pretends to be angry. They tussle in a friendly fashion. They are enjoying the day's warmth, the shade of the apple trees, the thick grass, the nearness of their masters.

"I turned the compost," he says, tipping his head back in relaxation. "It looks really good. All black and smelly."

"Excellent," I enthuse, meaning it. My back doesn't allow for turning compost.

"Yeah," he continues, "and the dogs keep stealing big, disgusting clumps of it and rolling in it. Chewing on it." He laughs, showing his straight, white teeth. I am reminded of how much I love him.

"Dogs are weird," I say, amused. We sip silently for a time.

"Honey," I say, "could you draw up a little landscape plan for me, for the north side of the house? You're so good at it. I'm good at making flowerbeds, growing stuff and all, but you're the one who's able to see the big picture." I pause hopefully. He nods.

"I can give it a shot," he says in his affable way, "this summer." I am pleased. He drew up the plan for our last house, and it was a great success. I know he will follow through. He always follows through.

He heads back to his vegetable garden, and the dogs frolic along behind him like spotted rocking horses. I think of all the gardening I do, then I think of all the gardening I could not do, if it weren't for him.

He is, of course, a most satisfactory husband.

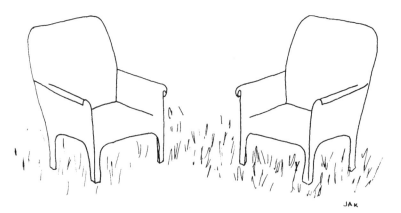

JAK

On Dog Days & Tough Mums

August is an annoying month for gardeners. It just seems as though all of the really good stuff finished blooming in May or June, when the sun was still kissing the flowers' sweet little upturned faces with a gentle touch. But now it's August, and the sun quit with the light kisses a long time ago. It wants to burn those babies!

Daylilies, old fashioned roses, columbines, and pinks are nobody's fools. Sure they laze prettily around during May and June; but as July nears they pack up their bags, cry "See ya!" to the still-snoring chrysanthemums, and hit the road. Good old Mother Sunshine becomes the Ugly Step-mother, and these late-spring, fair-weather friends have no intention of sticking around to sweep up ashes.

So, who do we have left? After all, somebody's got to take up where the heat-shy lovelies left off. We need the tough guys now. And believe me, they're up for it.

The brawny mums (*Chrysanthemum*) are only too happy to oblige, and don't turn your nose up at their old-fashioned familiarity. They come in nearly every color of the rainbow now, ranging from cute miniatures to hulking, four-foot giants. The hardy Dahlia (*D. compositae*) is no slouch either. I've got some beefy ones leaning mightily against my garage wall; they're six-feet tall if they're an inch. I don't even bother digging up their tubers in the fall. They're so tough even the slugs give them a wide berth. They frighten me sometimes, too; I mean, it's as though they take August's heat, slap it around a little, and just keep getting bigger. Next year I expect they'll be wearing leather jackets and shouting "Hey, mama" to me as I pass by. Tough.

The yard-high Phlox (*P. decussata*) is ready to do business in August, too. Like a giant sweet william, it stares the sun directly in the eye and says, "Bring it on, I love it!" Pink Daisies (*Dendranthema rubella* 'Clara Curtis') are the same—none of that wimpy shade for them. Black-Eyed Susan (*Rudbeckia fulgida*) is simply breathtaking in August when planted in drifts on a sunny wall; the sky blue Pincushion Flower *(Scabiosa caucasica* 'Perfecta') adds a vivid sweetness to a hot and tired perennial bed, and chipper pink Coreopsis *(C. rosea)* blooms so profusely in the hot, late-summer sun that you will stop, scratch your head, and try to remember if you really planted quite that many of them.

Just for fun, you can also try the bushy, fragrant, and loudly scarlet Red Valerian *(Centranthus ruber),* the shocking hot-pink Obedience Plant *(Physotegia virginiana),* the snowball-festooned Achillea *(A. ptarmatica* 'The Pearl'), some lavender-blue Asters (*Aster x Frikartii* 'Wonder of Staffa'), or ropes and ropes of climbing clematis, a lush vine that will turn your homely old fence into a late-summer arbor.

All of these perennials thrive in August, which means you need to take a good, hard look at your flowerbeds now, make a list, and plant either this fall or next spring so that next August won't find your yard looking so grim. And remember, be bold. Mother Nature's colors do not clash.

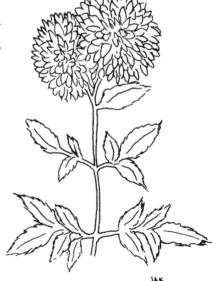

Although, if you have any big, tough, dahlias hanging around your garage, picking their teeth with your tomato stakes and blocking your

JAK

daisies' sun, be careful about what innocent little plant you put next to them. And don't look them in the eye. You don't want to attract their attention.

Absence *makes the* Yard Grow Harder

eptember. I sigh with relief as I watch the children climb aboard the bus once more, and sigh again, in near defeat, as I look at all the damage to my house and yard that I will now have time to repair.

I've been busy this summer with children—trying to keep them busy and television free—with remodeling projects in our old house, with in-laws who came for a jolly visit, with destructive dogs, with writing, and with whatever small amount of gardening I could squeeze in. And I'm talking a very small amount of gardening. My poor yard and gardens were delegated to the bottom of the priority list this summer, and it shows.

For starters, my grass is dead. I vowed I would install an in-ground, automatic sprinkler system this year, and in lieu of that, I would at least set out the old hose sprinkler, but it never happened. My lawn looks like a UFO launching pad.

My rose border, which I mulched heavily last spring in anticipation of a busy summer, is nevertheless choked with Joe-Pye weed, chickweed, and sea mallow. The border backs up against my neighbor's fence, and his weeds creep right under it if I'm not there daily, flailing away.

My dahlias, which I didn't stake well enough, have fallen over. One can no longer walk on the sidewalk next to them without tripping over them, poor souls.

Apples are dropping off the trees in the orchard. We simply have too many.

I have allowed the mint to have its way in the herb patch. In two years it has grown from a cunning little sprig to something resembling a dead tumbleweed. It has surrounded and captured its sad neighbors, demanding ransom for their release. However, in the best American fashion, I will pay no ransom; I shall simply wade in, dressed in riot gear, wielding a shovel and a garden weasel. Teresa Keene does not negotiate!

On the other hand, during key, quiet moments this summer, I did manage to keep the flowers watered. I weeded the flower borders by the driveway an astounding two times, and with their heavy mulch that was enough. I saw the poppy seeds I had scattered next to the potting shed come to fruition, and that was beautiful. Their red and pink heads bobbed nicely for most of the summer, and they did not want nor need my puny assistance.

And really, come to think of it, the whole shebang looked pretty darn good until a couple of weeks ago, and that's an accomplishment, really. You see, I have a system. In the fall, I plant bulbs, pull weeds, and mulch. In the winter, I read seed catalogs, prune, and mulch. The cool weather is better for hard work like this. In the spring, I plant seedlings, weed, make new flower beds, feed the lawn, and mulch. And in the summer, I hope that the work I have done during the other three seasons will pay off, allowing my charges to go it on their own for the most part. And they do! That is until early September, when they are ready for me to lend a helping hand once more.

And, by then, I, too, am ready to do so, my interest in them revitalized by the welcome break. Once again, they are no longer a chore, but a joy.

The Compelling Allure *of* Bulbs

I f one is a child, October means Halloween and candy and jack-o'-lanterns. If one is a New Englander, it means a big, grand, splashy show of color as the leaves turn red and yellow and orange. If one is a Southerner, October can still feel like summertime. But if one is a gardener, it means only one thing.

Bulbs!

Once again, October finds me waiting by the window, watching for the UPS man. I dare not go away for a weekend; he'll leave the box on the front porch and the bulbs might rot or get stolen! I must not start a project I cannot interrupt, lest the bulbs sit impatiently in my potting shed, calling out their siren song to me: Plant us, plant us! You know you want to! It will take hours and hours to do the job, so you'd better start now! There might be an early freeze! Disaster! Plant us!

The UPS man comes, and I rush to meet him like a wife whose husband has returned from war. The beginnings of a smile curve his lips; he is flattered that a woman is rushing toward him, smiling ecstatically. His smile turns to a puzzled frown as I snatch the box rudely away and hasten back into my house, robe flapping behind me. He drives off in a huff. Just another overeager customer.

I fetch my handy-dandy pocket knife (also good for slicing suckers off trees), and carefully slice through the tape. A mountain of bagged bulbs greets my eye, and suddenly I feel jealous, miserly. I am Ebenezer Scrooge hovering hoardishly over my pile of organic gold. I cackle gleefully. Mine, all mine!

I leap into my gardening togs and look out the window. Once again, the weather has conspired to bring torrents of rain down around my property, as it does every year when my bulbs arrive. This does not deter me, however. I hoist my box and head out.

I have a bed prepared just for this purpose. It is a new perennial bed next to the driveway, and it is turned, seasoned, and composted. It is ready to receive my offerings. I lay the globular bits of promise around in the bed. Tall in back—that would be the seven-foot asiatic lilies in the cream and yellow shades. I leave room between them. I want to plant some sunflowers there next spring. Smaller lilies, daffodils, tulips, crocus, muscari, and more; they all go in. I am drenched with rain and perspiration, but couldn't care less. I ordered the bulbs last spring, in a fever of hot desire, and now I plant them the same way. I leave lots of room between each. Soon a shipment of perennial seedlings will arrive, and they will go in, too. After all, one must have something blooming after the spring bulbs are done.

Many hours later, I finish. I am tired now. My boots are full of water. My gloves are sodden and black. My back hurts. I've worn through the knees of my pants. My hair is plastered to my head and neck. My mascara has dripped off my chin. I feel hot and dirty and soaking wet and tired.

But my bulbs have come, and are in! Next spring will reveal a hitherto unknown display of color in a spot previously dead and dull!

I am well pleased.

The November Blues

ain and sleet slash threateningly down my window panes, and I sit in my big wing chair, watching. I am comfortable. I have a big mug of coffee in my hand. My feet are up on a soft footstool. My housework is done and I have the rest of the day to work on my novel. I have all the lights blazing in the house today, for I am missing the sun and am trying to duplicate its warm glow.

But I miss my flowers.

I know I should go to my office and do some work. Much needs to be done. But I can't seem to do it. I simply want to look out the window and remember what my garden used to look like, before this harsh weather took over. I want to imagine what the garden will look like after this weather has passed. I am desolate today for some reason.

There is only one cure for the November gardener's blues: seed catalogs.

Delighted with the idea, I scurry into my bedroom and rummage through the closet, finally pulling from the back the large cardboard box that I have been throwing catalogs into for years. Treasure! I am ecstatic. I haul it back to my chair in the living room, tuck my feet under myself and dig in. Irises, in blues and pinks, whites and yellows! Roses! Climbing roses, tea roses, grandifloras, ramblers, miniatures! Daffodils! 'King Alfreds!' Tulips! Heather! Lavender! Irish moss! Trumpet vines! Honeysuckle, astilbe, lady ferns, daisies, lamb's ears, dahlias, yarrow!

The order form!

I know I shouldn't. Now is not a good time! It's like grocery shopping when you're hungry! Strike that—starving! I leap up and search for a pen. My checkbook fairly flies into my hand. I order in a feeding frenzy. Too much! Too much! But what should I cross out? I am helpless in the grip of the November Blues-Seed Catalog monster, and I couldn't be happier. I put the envelope in my mailbox, sated.

Now I can get some work done!

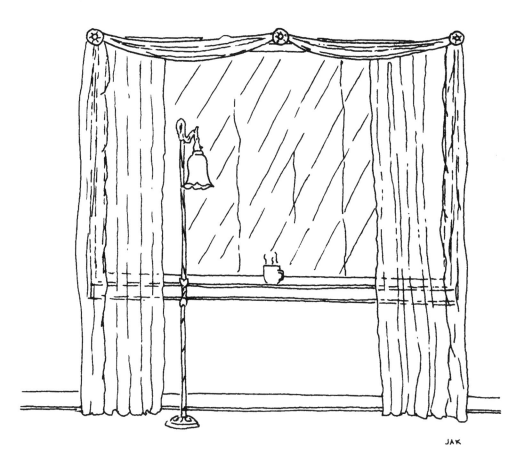

JAK

On Wishing One Could Change *the* Past

It is cold here in my little office. It is morning still, and the ancient leviathan that we laughingly call our furnace has yet to push its warm air all the way up to the third floor of the house. It sits in dampness down there in the chilly basement, where water bubbles up through the cracks in the cement floor as the water table rises. Rain, melting snow, and swelling underground streams all conspire against my deep-set basement. It is a bathtub.

My mind wanders, and worries for my garden prevail. Does the dahlia and lily bed have enough drainage? For many of us, the hardpan lies so close to the surface that our flower beds are planted in only one to one and one-half feet of topsoil. The bed, without good drainage built in, can become a bathtub just like my basement, holding in water and drowning the roots of our perennials. Factor this in while digging new beds. Dig a trough away from the bed, sloping downwards if possible, put a few inches of gravel in it, and cover it back up with dirt. Ideally, this will drain much of the water away from your plants' tender roots. It's a lot of extra work, but why bother digging the bed in the first place if the plants are going to be spoiled?

But I can't worry about drainage right now. What's done is done and December is several months too late to try to change things. I will hope for the best and make corrections in the spring if necessary. Right now I worry about the bulbs in my orchard. Last fall I lifted many hundreds of pieces of sod, placing daffodils, crocus, and muscari directly underneath. As I had hoped and dreamed, spring brought a glorious display under the white and pink blossoms of my 'King,' 'Transparent,' and 'McIntosh' trees, all golden and azure and royal purple. But I fear that I was impatient; as the blooms faded and the bulbs' leaves endured, I became increasingly frustrated with the shabby, unmown appearance of my pretty arbor.

Yes, yes, I know that one must let bulb greens die back naturally before cutting them down so the leaves can collect nourishment from the sun and feed the bulbs for a good show next spring. But June was at hand and the leaves were only one-half to three-quarters brown when I lost patience and mowed them down. Should I have waited another week or two? Will my haste affect the spring display? I kick myself now, but I know I'd probably do it again.

I look at my skeletonlike trees and see the mistakes made in earlier pruning attempts. This spring I will make sure the pruning is done before the trees leaf out, ensuring that my trees are better looking in their naked-ness next winter.

My office is warmer. Circulation has returned to my toes and fingers, and the blood tingles near the surface, making me feel more lively and ready to go outside. I imagine that my old furnace has simulated spring in its way, bringing warmth to the cold branches that are my feet and hands and rushing the sap throughout my body. I am ready to leaf out, in a manner of speaking. The garden, though cold and spare, still has the power to beckon.

Index